ISBN - 13-978-1-7331481-5-3

INTRODUCTION

The Commissioned Translated Book of Matthew, The King James Version 1611

The Precept Study Bible Version books of 1 and 2 Esdras is the 40 and 41 first completed books from the 81 Bible book series; which contains precepts and appellations. This version has King James approval texts, with the additions of precepts of the Old Testament, the Apocrypha, and the New Testament books.

This version is the most accurate English translations in existence today, other versions of this texts part of the canonization versions, published by Christians and Jewish authorities. The methodology behind the Canon was to establish a process of theories and beliefs of God: personal interpretations. The Cannon committee later concluded which books from the 81 to be part of that process for public ownership and books of study. Their self-will authority of canonization, the Cannon committee first removed many words from the Bible, including entire verses. Those can be found in many Bible publications today under the names of NIV, ESV, NLT, NKJV, including many others. The God of Israel inspires all scripture, and it was His spirit that gathers them; [**Isaiah 34:16** Seek ye out of the book of the LORD, and read: no one of these shall fail, none shall want her mate: for my mouth, it hath commanded, and his spirit it hath gathered them.

Hence, if any man diminishes from or add to it, The Most High God will take away his part from the book of life [**Deuteronomy 4:2** Ye shall not add unto the word which I command you, neither shall you diminish ought from it, that ye may keep the commandments of the Lord your God which I command you.

Deuteronomy 12:32 What thing soever I command you, observe to do it: thou shalt not add thereto, nor diminish from it.

2

Revelation 22:19 and if any man shall take away from the words of the book of this prophecy, God shall take away his part out of the book of life, and out of the holy city, and from the things which are written in this book.]

Nevertheless, the Cannon committee authorized and removed all the Apocrypha books from the Bible, which would intentionally remove many precepts within there for understanding other sections of the Bible. However, the removal of the Apocrypha gave the reader false understandings such as The Most High God was silent for four hundred years. People today call it the Gap Theory. The Apocrypha would have shown the reader that Jesus shall be revealed within four hundred years; [**2 Esdras 7:28** For my son Jesus shall be revealed with those that be with him, and they that remain shall rejoice within four hundred years.]

However, with the removal of the Apocrypha, today, much of the world believes that The Most High God was silent for four hundred years. Another massive confusion with the removal of the Apocrypha is the Gentiles became part of the covenant The Most High God made with the Jacob, and all the children from him would be called Israelites. The book of 1 Maccabees gives you the reason and thoughts why after coming out of the Greek captivity, many believed they were Greeks/Grecian; Hellenists.

[**1 Maccabees 1:41** Moreover king Antiochus wrote to his whole kingdom, that all should be one people.] Later that became law. If anyone was found with the book of the law, even practicing the way of The God of Israel, and not profaning the sabbath days, will die. That is why Paul makes the statement in [**Galatians 3:28** There is neither Jew nor Greek, there is neither bond nor free, there is neither male nor female: for ye are all one in Christ Jesus.]

However, Paul makes its clear who he preached the gospel to in [**Acts 26:6-7** And now I stand and am judged for the hope of the promise made of God unto our fathers: 7 unto which promise our twelve tribes, instantly serving God day and night, hope to come. For which hopes sake, king Agrippa, I am accused of the Jews.]

One should see the importance of scripture being removed, making the reader unable to bridge from the Old Testament to the New Testament section. The Cannon committee sights were also focused on other books to be included in the removal process. Martin Luther was endangering the removal from the Old and New Testament books. For example, he famously wanted Hebrews, James, Jude, and Revelation removed from the Bible during the Canonization process Because of his beliefs. Including the books of Esther, Proverbs, Ecclesiastes, Song of Songs, and Ezekiel from the Old Testament.

The primary purpose of The Precept Study Bible Version series and its separation of book, it will give the reader a better and more authentic experience of how to focus, and study as our forefather's study scripture writings we know witness within the Bible texts. However, today, Bibles are contained as one volume of collected books for distribution to a broader audience. Like King James, the I and the VI felt it was necessary making it more difficult to destroy by rulers and kings of this world today. Initially, King James commissioned and authorized 81 books for translations, which also contained the book of Matthew. Except precepts and appellations added by me, Elder Michael Johnson, Sr. The Precept Study Bible is in its original English translation, King James commissioned over 400 years ago.

Hence, The Precept Study Bible Version series contains no references, only precepts and appellations for an understanding of the time it was written. One must remember the Christian and Jewish communities will attempt to keep the studier seeking their methods and theories for their knowledge about God. Sad to say, today Christian doctrine is the leading conglomerate, which is the influence to more than 40 thousands plus doctrines of theories around the world today. Anyone using the methods of theological studies, using the Christians methodology will take the approach using Hermeneutics, Exegesis, and Inductive Bible study methods. Those methods interpret scripture, with personal conclusions, interpretations a religious worldview not perceptual understanding of the scriptures.

To study using Precepts is not a method trying to influence your thoughts, positions, understandings, or views using a personal approach. According to Scripture, the Bible says in [**Isaiah 28:10** For precept must be upon precept, precept upon precept; Line upon line, line upon line; Here a little, and there a little:

Psalm 119:4 Thou hast commanded us To keep thy precepts diligently.

Psalm 119:104 Through thy precepts I get Understanding: Therefore I hate every false way.]

The Bible only speaks of using precepts, not Hermeneutics, Exegesis, or Inductive study methods. My intentions are for the reader to better understand what The Most High God of Israel requires them to inherit eternal life using only Bible precepts and appellations.

Thank you for the purchase of this book, and may The Most High God indeed bless you with His knowledge and understanding.

This book is dedicated to my beloved mother, brother, grandfather, and grandmother: my mother Gloria Reed, brother Melvin Johnson ("D"), grandfather Johnnie Ransom (PaPa), and grandmother Ivy Ransom (MoMo). I loved them all very much, in hopes to see them in New Jerusalem.

1 ESDRAS

1 ESDRAS CHAPTER 1

1 And Josias held *the feast of* the passover in Jerusalem unto his Lord, and offered the passover the fourteenth day of the first month;
*Precept: Josias = Joh-SIGH-uhs is the Greek translation. The Hebrew name is **Josiah** = Joh-SIGH-uh; means: The root of this comes from "Yahawah brings forth, to heal: 2 Kings 21:23-24 | **Passover**: Exodus 12:5-6 | Leviticus 23:5 | Numbers 9:5; 28:16 | Joshua 5:10 | Ezra 6:19*

2 having set the priests according to *their* daily courses, being arrayed in long garments, in the temple of the Lord.
Precept: Priests = Called Ministers

3 And he spake unto the Levites, the holy ministers of Israel, that *they* should hallow themselves unto the Lord, to set the holy ark of the Lord in the house that king Solomon the *son* of David had built:
*Precept: Solomon = SAHL-uh-muhn; means: Will give Shalom, The LORD's beloved | **Israel** = IZ-ray-el; means: A prince of God | **Ministers** = Called Priests: Joel 1:9, 13 | Numbers 3:3 | Ezra 8:17 | Psalm 103:21*

4 *and said,* Ye shall no more bear the ark upon your shoulders: now therefore serve the Lord your God, and minister unto his people Israel, and prepare you after your families and kindreds,
*Precept: The Tribe of Levi was the ones to bear the ark: Deuteronomy 10:8 | **Israel** = IZ-ray-el; means: A prince of God*

5 according as David the king of Israel prescribed, and according to the magnificence of Solomon his son: and standing in the temple according to the several dignity of the families of you the Levites, who *minister* in the presence of your brethren the children of Israel,
*Precept: Solomon = SAHL-uh-muhn; means: Will give Shalom, The LORD's beloved | **Israel** = IZ-ray-el; means: A prince of God | **Prescribed** = Directed, or Ordered |*

Brethren = breth-ran: means: Referring to the members of a Sect, society, or of Profession. Many times used as Brother: Genesis 9:22, 25; 19:7 | Deuteronomy 3:20; 10:9 | 1 Esdras 8:47 | Tobit 1:3

6 offer the passover in order, and make ready the sacrifices for your brethren, and keep the passover according to the commandment of the Lord, which was given unto Moses.

Precept: Passover*: Exodus 12:5-6 | Leviticus 23:5 | Numbers 9:5; 28:16 | Joshua 5:10 | Ezra 6:19 | **Sacrifice** = Prepare; Practice: Genesis 27:17 | Exodus 12:39; 15:2; 23:20 | Numbers 15:5-6; 23:1, 29 | Joshua 1:11 | Psalms 103:9 | Proverbs 8:27 | Jonah 4:6-7 | 1 Esdras 1:13-14 | 2 Esdras 8:60; 9:18 | Practice: Sirach/Ecclesiasticus 10:6 | 2 Peter 2:14 | **Brethren** = breth-ran: means: Referring to the members of a Sect, society, or of Profession. Many times used as Brother: Genesis 9:22, 25; 19:7 | Deuteronomy 3:20; 10:9 | 1 Esdras 8:47 | Tobit 1:3*

7 And unto the people that was found *there* Josias gave thirty thousand lambs *and* kids, and three thousand calves: these *things* were given of the king's *allowance*, according as *he* promised, to the people, to the priests, and to the Levites.

Precept: Josias *= Joh-SIGH-uhs is the Greek translation. The Hebrew name is **Josiah** = Joh-SIGH-uh; means: The root of this comes from "Yahawah brings forth, to heal: 2 Kings 21:23-24 | **Priests** = Called Ministers*

8 And Helkias, Zacharias, and Syelus, the governors of the temple, gave to the priests for the passover two thousand and six hundred sheep, *and* three hundred calves.

Precept: Helkias *= hehl-KIGH-uhs is Greek. The Hebrew translation of **Shallum** = SHAL-uhm; means: The requited, The replaced: Ezra 2:42; 7:2; 10:24 | **Zacharias** = ZAK-uh-RIGH-uhs; means: Yahweh remembers | **Passover**: Exodus 12:5-6 | Leviticus 23:5 | Numbers 9:5; 28:16 | Joshua 5:10 | Ezra 6:19 | **Syelus** = such-EE-luhs is the Greek translation. The Hebrew name is **Jehiel** = Jim-HIGH-el; means: may God live, Yahawah living one: 1 Chronicles 9:35 | Ezra 8:9; 10:2 | **Priests** = Called Ministers*

9 And Jeconias, and Samaias, and Nathanael *his* brother, and Assabias, and Ochiel, and Joram, captains over thousands, gave to the Levites for the passover five thousand sheep, *and* seven hundred calves.

Precept: Jeconias *= Jew-oj-NIGH-uhs is the Greek translation. The Hebrew name is **Jeconiah** = Jew-oh-NIGH-uh; means: Whom Yahawah establishes: 1 Chronicles 3:16-17 | Esther 2:6 | Jeremiah 24:1 | **Nathanael** = nut-THAN-ay-uhl; means: Gift of God | **Assabias** = ass-uh-Bigh-uhs, is the Greek translation. The Hebrew name is **Hashabiah** = HASH-uh-BIgH-uh; means: 1 Chronicles 6:45 | Ezra 8:19, 24 |*

Nehemiah 11:22 | **Ochiel** = oh-KIGH-el is the Greek translation. The Hebrew name is **Jeiel** = Jim-IGH; means: Yahawah is strong: 1 Chronicles 5:7; 15:18, 21 | Ezra 8:13; 10:43 | **Joram** = JOH-ruhm is also spelled **Jehoram** = Jim-HOH-ruhm; means: Yahawah is exalted: 2 Samuel 8:10 | 2 kings 8:16, 21 | 1 Chronicles 3:11 | **Jehoram**: 1 Kings 22:50 | 2 Chronicles 17:8 | **Passover**: Exodus 12:5-6 | Leviticus 23:5 | Numbers 9:5; 28:16 | Joshua 5:10 | Ezra 6:19 | **Samaias** = such-MAY-yuhs. The Hebrew translation is **Shemaiah** = shih-MAY-yuh; means: The LORD has heard: 1 Kings 12:22

10 And when these *things* were done, the priests and Levites, having the unleavened bread, stood in very comely order according to the kindreds,
Precept: Priests = Called Ministers

11 And according to the several dignities of the fathers, before the people, to offer to the Lord, as it is written in the book of Moses: and thus *did they* in the morning.
Precept: Dignities = dig-ni-tiz; means Glorious ones, What honor, Preeminent in power: Genesis 49:3 | Esther 6:3 | Ecclesiastes 10:6 | 2 Peter 2:10

12 And they roasted the passover with fire, as appertaineth: as for the sacrifices, they sod them in brass pots and pans with a good savour,
Precept: Passover: Exodus 12:5-6 | Leviticus 23:5 | Numbers 9:5; 28:16 | Joshua 5:10 | Ezra 6:19 | **Appertaineth/Appertain** = ap-er-tan; means: Only once, It becometh, It is seemly, pertain, and It is Thy honor: Jeremiah 10:7 | Leviticus 6:5 | Nehemiah 2:8 | **Sacrifice** = Prepare; Practice: Genesis 27:17 | Exodus 12:39; 15:2; 23:20 | Numbers 15:5-6; 23:1, 29 | Joshua 1:11 | Psalms 103:9 | Proverbs 8:27 | Jonah 4:6-7 | 1 Esdras 1:13-14 | 2 Esdras 8:60; 9:18 | Practice: Sirach/Ecclesiasticus 10:6 | 2 Peter 2:14

13 and set *them* before all the people: and afterward they prepared for themselves, and for the priests their brethren, the sons of Aaron.
Precept: Priests = Called Ministers | **Brethren** = breth-ran: means: Referring to the members of a Sect, society, or of Profession. Many times used as Brother: Genesis 9:22, 25; 19:7 | Deuteronomy 3:20; 10:9 | 1 Esdras 8:47 | Tobit 1:3

14 For the priests offered the fat until night: and the Levites prepared for themselves, and the priests their brethren, the sons of Aaron.
Precept: Brethren = breth-ran: means: Referring to the members of a Sect, society, or of Profession. Many times used as Brother: Genesis 9:22, 25; 19:7 | Deuteronomy

3:20; 10:9 | 1 Esdras 8:47 | Tobit 1:3

15 The holy singers also, the sons of Asaph, were in their order, according to the appointment of David, to wit, Asaph, Zacharias, and Jeduthun, who was of the king's retinue.

Precept: Asaph = AY-saf; means: He collected | Zacharias = ZAK-uh-RIGH-uhs; means: Yahweh remembers | Jeduthun = jih-DYOO-thuhn; means: Praise | David = DAY-vid. The name David is a suggested title to the throne, not a personal name; means: The True Messiah | Priests = Called Ministers

16 Moreover the porters *were* at every gate; it was not lawful for any to go from his ordinary service: for their brethren the Levites prepared for them.

Precept: Brethren = breth-ran: means: Referring to the members of a Sect, society, or of Profession. Many times used as Brother: Genesis 9:22, 25; 19:7 | Deuteronomy 3:20; 10:9 | 1 Esdras 8:47 | Tobit 1:3

17 Thus were the *things* that belonged to the sacrifices of the Lord accomplished in that day, that *they* might hold the passover,

Precept: Passover: Exodus 12:5-6 | Leviticus 23:5 | Sacrifice = Prepare; Practice: Genesis 27:17 | Exodus 12:39; 15:2; 23:20 | Numbers 15:5-6; 23:1, 29 | Joshua 1:11 | Psalms 103:9 | Proverbs 8:27 | Jonah 4:6-7 | 1 Esdras 1:13-14 | 2 Esdras 8:60; 9:18 | Practice: Sirach/Ecclesiasticus 10:6 | 2 Peter 2:14

18 and offer sacrifices upon the altar of the Lord, according to the commandment of king Josias.

Precept: Josias = Joh-SIGH-uhs is the Greek translation. The Hebrew name is Josiah = Joh-SIGH-uh; means: The root of this comes from "Yahawah brings forth, to heal: 2 Kings 21:23-24 | Sacrifice = Prepare; Practice: Genesis 27:17 | Exodus 12:39; 15:2; 23:20 | Numbers 15:5-6; 23:1, 29 | Joshua 1:11 | Psalms 103:9 | Proverbs 8:27 | Jonah 4:6-7 | 1 Esdras 1:13-14 | 2 Esdras 8:60; 9:18 | Practice: Sirach/Ecclesiasticus 10:6 | 2 Peter 2:14

19 So the children of Israel which were present held the passover at that time, and the feast of sweet bread seven days.

Precept: Passover: Exodus 12:5-6 | Leviticus 23:5 | Numbers 9:5; 28:16 | Israel = IZ-ray-el; means: A prince of God

20 And such a passover was not kept in Israel since the time of the prophet Samuel.

Precept: Passover: Exodus 12:5-6 | Leviticus 23:5 | Numbers 9:5; 28:16 | Joshua 5:10 | Ezra 6:19 | Prophet = A prophet of God is one who has authority and who has the

qualifications to convey God's messages to men. Being God's mouth piece. A prophet interpret scripture Parables, Riddles, and dark speeches, giving one the Oracles and the mystery of God word: Jeremiah 3:15; 44:4 | 2 Kings 17:13 | 1 Chronicles 16:22 | Psalms 105:15 | 2 Esdras 1:32 | Matthew 13:35 | **Israel** = IZ-ray-el; means: A prince of God

21 Yea, all the kings of Israel held not such a passover as Josias, and the priests, and the Levites, and the Jews, held with all Israel that were found dwelling at Jerusalem.

Precept: Passover: Exodus 12:5-6 | Leviticus 23:5 | Numbers 9:5; 28:16 | Joshua 5:10 | Ezra 6:19 | **Israel** = IZ-ray-el; means: A prince of God | **Priests** = Called Ministers | **Josias** = Joh-SIGH-uhs is the Greek translation. The Hebrew name is **Josiah** = Joh-SIGH-uh; means: The root of this comes from "Yahawah brings forth, to heal: 2 Kings 21:23-24

22 In the eighteenth year of the reign of Josias was this passover kept.

Precept: Josias = Joh-SIGH-uhs is the Greek translation. The Hebrew name is **Josiah** = Joh-SIGH-uh; means: The root of this comes from "Yahawah brings forth, to heal: 2 Kings 21:23-24 | **Passover**: Exodus 12:5-6 | Leviticus 23:5 | Numbers 9:5; 28:16 | Joshua 5:10 | Ezra 6:19

23 And the works or Josias were upright before his Lord with an heart full of godliness.

Precept: Josias = Joh-SIGH-uhs is the Greek translation. The Hebrew name is **Josiah** = Joh-SIGH-uh; means: The root of this comes from "Yahawah brings forth, to heal: 2 Kings 21:23-24

24 As for the *things* that came to pass in his time, they were written in former times, concerning those that sinned, and did wickedly against the Lord above all people and kingdoms, and how they grieved him exceedingly, so that the words of the Lord rose up against Israel.

Precept: Sinned = Disobedience, Evil, Transgression of God law, Wickedness, Rebellious against The Most High God: Genesis 39:9 | 1 John 3:4 | **Grieved** = Angered, or burden | **Israel** = IZ-ray-el; means: A prince of God

25 Now after all these acts of Josias it came to pass, that Pharaoh the king of Egypt came to raise war at Carchamis upon Euphrates: and Josias went out against him.

Precept: Josias = Joh-SIGH-uhs is the Greek translation. The Hebrew name is **Josiah** = Joh-SIGH-uh; means: The root of this comes from "Yahawah brings forth, to heal: 2

Kings 21:23-24 | **Carchamis** = *Charchemish, is the West Bank of the upper Euphrates River: 2 Chronicles 35:20* | **Euphrates** = *you-FRAY-teez*

26 But the king of Egypt sent to him, saying, What have I to do with thee, O king of Judea?
*Precept: **Judea** = joo-DEE-uh; means: Jew*

27 I am not sent out from the Lord God against thee; for my war is upon Euphrates: and now the Lord is with me, yea, the Lord is with *me* hasting me forward: depart from *me*, and be not against the Lord.
*Precept: **Euphrates** = you-FRAY-teez*

28 Howbeit Josias did not turn back his chariot from him, but undertook to fight with him, not regarding the words of the prophet Jeremy *spoken* by the mouth of the Lord:
*Precept: **Jeremy** = Jeremiah | **Josias** = Joh-SIGH-uhs is the Greek translation. The Hebrew name is **Josiah** = Joh-SIGH-uh; means: The root of this comes from "Yahawah brings forth, to heal: 2 Kings 21:23-24*

29 but joined battle with him in the plain of Magiddo, and the princes came against king Josias.
*Precept: **Josias** = Joh-SIGH-uhs is the Greek translation. The Hebrew name is **Josiah** = Joh-SIGH-uh; means: The root of this comes from "Yahawah brings forth, to heal: 2 Kings 21:23-24 | **The plain of Magiddo** is located in the Jezreel valley of Northern Jerusalem: 2 Kings 23:29, 30 | 2 Chronicles 35:20-27*

30 Then said the king unto his servants, Carry me away out of the battle; for I am very weak. And immediately his servants took him away out of the battle.

31 Then gat he up upon his second chariot; and being brought back to Jerusalem died, and was buried in his father's sepulchre.

32 And in all Jewry they mourned for Josias, yea, Jeremy the prophet lamented for Josias, and the chief *men* with the women made lamentation for him unto this day: and this was given out *for an ordinance* to be done continually in all the nation of Israel.
*Precept: **Josias** = Joh-SIGH-uhs is the Greek translation. The Hebrew name is **Josiah***

11

*= Joh-SIGH-uh; means: The root of this comes from "Yahawah brings forth, to heal: 2 Kings 21:23-24 | **Jeremy** = Jeremiah | **Jewry** = The country of Judea, Judah: Daniel 5:13 | Luke 23:5 | John 7:1 | **Israel** = IZ-ray-el; means: A prince of God | **Parallel Passage**: Matthew 1:11 | **Parallel verse**: 2 Chronicles 35:25*

33 These *things* are written in the book of the stories of the kings of Judah, and every one of the acts that Josias did, and his glory, and his understanding in the law of the Lord, and the *things* that he had done before, and the *things* now *recited*, are reported in the book of the kings of Israel and Judea.
*Precept: **Judea** = The country of Jewry, County of the Jews: Ezra 5:8 | 1 Esdras 1:26; 2:5, 12 | Tobit 1:18 | Judith 1:12 | 1 Maccabees 4:35 | Matthew 2:5 | **Josias** = Joh-SIGH-uhs is the Greek translation. The Hebrew name is **Josiah** = Joh-SIGH-uh; means: The root of this comes from "Yahawah brings forth, to heal: 2 Kings 21:23-24 | **Israel** = IZ-ray-el; means: A prince of God*

34 And the people took Joachaz the son of Josias, and made *him* king instead of Josias his father, when he was twenty and three years old.
*Precept: **Josias** = Joh-SIGH-uhs is the Greek translation. The Hebrew name is **Josiah** = Joh-SIGH-uh; means: The root of this comes from "Yahawah brings forth, to heal: 2 Kings 21:23-24 | **Joachaz** = JOH-uh-kaz; means: The LORD has grasped | **Parallel**: 2 Kings 23:30*

35 And he reigned in Judea and in Jerusalem three months: and *then* the king of Egypt deposed him from reigning in Jerusalem.
*Precept: **Judea** = The country of Jewry, County of the Jews: Ezra 5:8 | 1 Esdras 1:26; 2:5, 12 | Tobit 1:18 | Judith 1:12 | 1 Maccabees 4:35 | Matthew 2:5*

36 And he set a tax upon the land of an hundred talents of silver and one talent of gold.

37 The king of Egypt also made king Joacim his brother king of Judea and Jerusalem.
*Precept: **Judea** = The country of Jewry, County of the Jews: Ezra 5:8 | 1 Esdras 1:26; 2:5, 12 | Tobit 1:18 | Judith 1:12 | 1 Maccabees 4:35 | Matthew 2:5*

38 And he bound Joacim and the nobles: but Zaraces his brother he apprehended, and brought him out of Egypt.
*Precept: **Joacim** = JOH-uh-kim | **Nobles** = well known, famous, highborn, Possessing eminence | **Zaraces** = ZEHR-uh-seez*

12

39 Five and twenty years old was Joacim when he was made king in the land of Judea and Jerusalem; and he did evil before the Lord.
Precept: Judea = The country of Jewry, County of the Jews: Ezra 5:8 | 1 Esdras 1:26; 2:5, 12 | Tobit 1:18 | Judith 1:12 | 1 Maccabees 4:35 | Matthew 2:5

40 Wherefore against him Nabuchodonosor the king of Babylon came up, and bound him with a chain of brass, and carried *him* into Babylon.
Precept: Nabuchodonosor = NAB-uh-kuh-DAHN-ub-sawr | Babylon = Confuse, Confound; An enormously important city in antiquity ("gate of the god") | Parallel: 2 Chronicles 36:6

41 Nabuchodonosor also took of the holy vessels of the Lord, and carried *them* away, and set them in his own temple at Babylon.
Precept: Nabuchodonosor = NAB-uh-kuh-DAHN-ub-sawr | Babylon = Confuse, Confound; An enormously important city in antiquity ("gate of the god")

42 But *those things* that are recorded of him, and *of* his uncleaness and impiety, are written in the chronicles of the kings.
Precept: Impiety = Scoffing, Ungodliness, Irreverence towards God, Neglect of the divine precepts, Disobedience to divine commands, Blasphemy

43 And Joacim his son reigned in his stead: he was made *king* being eighteen years old;
Precept: Joacim = JOH-uh-kim | Parallel: 2 Kings 24:8 | 2 Chronicles 36:9

44 and reigned *but* three months and ten days in Jerusalem; and did evil before the Lord.

45 So after a year Nabuchodonosor sent and caused him to be brought into Babylon with the holy vessels of the Lord;
Precept: Nabuchodonosor = NAB-uh-kuh-DAHN-ub-sawr | Babylon = Confuse, Confound; An enormously important city in antiquity ("gate of the god")

46 and made Zedechias king of Judea and Jerusalem, when he was one and twenty years old; and he reigned eleven years:

*Precept: **Judea*** = *The country of Jewry, County of the Jews: Ezra 5:8 | 1 Esdras 1:26; 2:5, 12 | Tobit 1:18 | Judith 1:12 | 1 Maccabees 4:35 | Matthew 2:5*

47 and he did evil *also* in the sight of the Lord, and cared not for the words that were spoken *unto him* by the prophet Jeremy from the mouth of the Lord.
*Precept: **Jeremy*** = *Jeremiah*

48 And after that king Nabuchodonosor had made him to swear by the name of the Lord, he forswore himself, and rebelled; and hardening his neck, his heart, he transgressed the laws of the Lord God of Israel.
*Precept: **Nabuchodonosor*** = *NAB-uh-kuh-DAHN-ub-sawr* | ***Israel*** = *IZ-ray-el; means: A prince of God*

49 The governors also of the people and of the priests did many things against the laws, and passed all the pollutions of all nations, and defiled the temple of the Lord, which was sanctified in Jerusalem.
*Precept: **Priests*** = *Called Ministers*

50 Nevertheless the God of their fathers sent by his messenger to call them back, because he spared them and his tabernacle *also*.

51 But they had his messengers in derision; and, *look*, when the Lord spake *unto them*, they made a sport of his prophets:
*Precept: **Derision*** = *Mock, Scron, laugh at, and Ridicule: Psalm 44:13; 79:4 | Ezekiel 23:32 | Hosea 7:16 | Job 30:1 | Wisdom 5:3*

52 so far forth, that he, being wroth with his people for their *great* ungodliness, commanded the kings of the Chaldees to come up against them;
*Precept: **Chaldees*** = *Chaldeans*

53 who slew their young men with the sword, *yea, even* within the compass of their holy temple, and spared neither young man nor maid, old man nor child, among them; for he delivered all into their hands.

54 And they took all the holy vessels of the Lord, *both* great and small, with the vessels of the ark of God, and the king's treasures, and carried *them* away into Babylon.
*Precept: **Babylon** = Confuse, Confound; An enormously important city in antiquity ("gate of the god")*

55 As for the house of the Lord, they burnt it, and brake down the walls of Jerusalem, and set fire upon her towers:

56 and as for her glorious *things*, they never ceased till they had consumed and brought them all to nought: and the people that were not slain with the sword he carried unto Babylon:
*Precept: **Babylon** = Confuse, Confound; An enormously important city in antiquity ("gate of the god")*

57 who became servants to him and his children, till the Persians reigned, to fulfil the word of the Lord *spoken* by the mouth of Jeremy:
*Precept: **Jeremy** = Jeremiah: Jeremiah 25:11; 29:10 | **Persians** = our-SHANZ: Country laying east of Mesopotamia (modern Iraq)*

58 Until the land had enjoyed her sabbaths, the whole time of her desolation shall she rest, until the full term of seventy years.
*Precept: 2 Chronicles 36:21 | **Desolation** = DES-O-lation = Loneliness, Sadness, Devastation, Ruin. Also called **Desolate**: Genesis 47:19 | Leviticus 26:34-35 | Isaiah 13:9 | 1 Esdras 1:58; 2:23*

1 ESDRAS CHAPTER 2

1 In the first year of Cyrus king of the Persians, that the word of the Lord might be accomplished, *that he had promised* by the mouth of Jeremy;
Precept: Jeremy = *Jeremiah* | ***Cyrus*** = *SIGH-ruhs* | ***Persians*** = *our-SHANZ: Country laying east of Mesopotamia (modern Iraq)*

2 the Lord raised up the spirit of Cyrus the king of the Persians, and he made proclamation through all his kingdom, and also by writing,
Precept: Cyrus = *SIGH-ruhs* | ***Proclamation*** = *Public Announcement* | ***Persians*** = *our-SHANZ: Country laying east of Mesopotamia (modern Iraq)*

3 saying, Thus saith Cyrus king of the Persians; The Lord of Israel, the most high Lord, hath made me king of the whole world,
Precept: Cyrus = *SIGH-ruhs* | ***Persians*** = *our-SHANZ: Country laying east of Mesopotamia (modern Iraq)* | ***Israel*** = *IZ-ray-el; means: A prince of God*

4 and commanded me to build him an house at Jerusalem in Jewry.
Precept: Jewry = *The country of Judea, Judah: Daniel 5:13 | Luke 23:5 | John 7:1*

5 If therefore there be any of you *that are* of his people, let the Lord, *even* his Lord, be with him, and let him go up to Jerusalem that is in Judea, and build the house of the Lord of Israel: *for* he is the Lord that dwelleth in Jerusalem.
Precept: Judea = *The country of Jewry, County of the Jews: Ezra 5:8 | 1 Esdras 1:26; 2:5, 12 | Tobit 1:18 | Judith 1:12 | 1 Maccabees 4:35 | Matthew 2:5 | **Israel** = IZ-ray-el; means: A prince of God*

6 Whosoever then dwell in the places about, let them help him, (those, *I say*, that are his neighbours) with gold, and with silver,
Precept: Neighbour(s) = *One who is a fellow Israelite, Members of a community united by divine covenant, law, and teachings, the Israelites' obligations to Yahawah (God): Exodus 2:13; 19:6; 22:25-26 | Leviticus 19:13, 15-17 | Deuteronomy 15:7-11 | 1 Samuel 28:17*

7 with gifts, with horses, and *with* cattle, and other *things*, which have been set forth by vow, for the temple of the Lord at Jerusalem.

8 Then the chief of the families of Judea and of the tribe of Benjamin stood *up*; the priests also, and the Levites, and all they whose mind the Lord had moved to go up, and to build an house for the Lord at Jerusalem,

Precept: Judea = *The country of Jewry, County of the Jews: Ezra 5:8 | 1 Esdras 1:26; 2:5, 12 | Tobit 1:18 | Judith 1:12 | 1 Maccabees 4:35 | Matthew 2:5 | Priests* = *Called Ministers*

9 and they that dwelt round about them, *and* helped *them* in all *things* with silver and gold, *with* horses and cattle, and with very many free gifts of a great number whose minds were stirred up *thereto.*

10 King Cyrus also brought forth the holy vessels, which Nabuchodonosor had carried away from Jerusalem, and had set *up* in his temple of idols.

Precept: Cyrus = *SIGH-ruhs | Nabuchodonosor* = *NAB-uh-kuh-DAHN-ub-sawr | Parallel: Ezra 1:7; 5:14*

11 Now when Cyrus king of the Persians had brought them forth, he delivered them to Mithridates his treasurer:

Precept: Cyrus = *SIGH-ruhs | Mithridates* = *MITH-rih-DAY-teez | Persians* = *our-SHANZ: Country laying east of Mesopotamia (modern Iraq)*

12 and by him they were delivered to Sanabassar the governor of Judea.

Precept: Judea = *The country of Jewry, County of the Jews: Ezra 5:8 | 1 Esdras 1:26; 2:5, 12 | Tobit 1:18 | Judith 1:12 | 1 Maccabees 4:35 | Matthew 2:5 | Sanabassar* = *SAN-uh-BASS-uhr*

13 And this was the number of them; A thousand golden cups, and a thousand of silver, censers of silver twenty nine, vials of gold thirty, and of silver two thousand four hundred and ten, and a thousand other vessels.

14 So all the vessels of gold and of silver, which were carried away, were five thousand four hundred threescore and nine.

15 These were brought back by Sanabassar, together with them of the captivity, from Babylon to Jerusalem.
Precept: Babylon = *Confuse, Confound; An enormously important city in antiquity ("gate of the god")* | *Sanabassar* = *SAN-uh-BASS-uhr*

16 But in the time of Artexerxes king of the Persians Belemus, and Mithridates, and Tabellius, and Rathumus, and Beeltethmus, and Semellius the secretary, with others that were in commission with them, dwelling in Samaria and other places, wrote unto him against them that dwelt in Judea and Jerusalem *these* letters following;
Precept: Judea = *The country of Jewry, County of the Jews: Ezra 5:8* | *1 Esdras 1:26; 2:5, 12* | *Tobit 1:18* | *Judith 1:12* | *1 Maccabees 4:35* | *Matthew 2:5* | *Artexerxes* = *ar-TAKS-urk'-sez* | *Belemus* = *BEL-uh-muhs* | *Mithridates* = *MITH-rih-DAY-teez* | *Tabellius* = *tub-BEL-ih-uhs* | *Rathumus* = *Rehum the chancellor: Ezra 4:8* | *Beeltethmus* = *BEE-el-TETH-muhs* | *Semellius* = *sih-MEL-ih-uhs* | *Persians* = *our-SHANZ: Country laying east of Mesopotamia (modern Iraq)*

17 To king Artexerxes *our* lord, Thy servants, Rathumus the story*writer*, and Semellius the scribe, and the rest of their council, and the judges that are in Celosyria and Phenice.
Precept: Artexerxes = *ar-TAKS-urk'-sez* | *Rathumus* = *Rehum the chancellor: Ezra 4:8* | *Semellius* = *sih-MEL-ih-uhs* | *Celosyria* = *SEE-loh-SIHR-ih-uh; A location. The eastern harbor of Corinth: Acts 18:18* | *Romans 16:1* | *Phenice* = *fig-NIGH-sih; A town with a harbor on the southern side Crete: Acts 27:12*

18 Be it now known to the lord king, that the Jews that are up from you to us, being come into Jerusalem, (*that* rebellious and wicked city,) do build the marketplaces, and repair the walls of it and do lay the foundation of the temple.
Precept: Rebellious = *Resistance, Rebellion, Opposition to authority, Disobedient, Rebelled: Joshua 22:22* | *1 Samuel 15:23* | *Job 34:37* | *Jeremiah 28:16; 29:32* | *1 Esdras 2:27*

19 Now if this city and the walls *thereof* be made up *again*, they will not only refuse to give tribute, but also rebel against kings.

Precept: Rebel = *Disobedient, Rebellious: Numbers 27:13-14 | Nehemiah 9:26 | Isaiah 1:20*

20 And forasmuch as the *things* pertaining to the temple are *now* in hand, we think it meet not to neglect such a matter,

21 But to speak unto *our* lord the king, to the intent that, if it be thy pleasure it may be sought out in the books of thy fathers:

22 And thou shalt find in the chronicles what is written concerning these *things*, and shalt understand that that city was rebellious, troubling both kings and cities:
Precept: Rebellious = *Resistance, Rebellion, Opposition to authority, Disobedient, Rebelled: Joshua 22:22 | 1 Samuel 15:23 | Job 34:37 | Jeremiah 28:16; 29:32 | 1 Esdras 2:27*

23 and *that* the Jews *were* rebellious, and raised always wars therein; for the which cause even this city was made desolate.
Precept: Rebellious = *Resistance, Rebellion, Opposition to authority, Disobedient, Rebelled: Joshua 22:22 | 1 Samuel 15:23 | Job 34:37 | Jeremiah 28:16; 29:32 | 1 Esdras 2:27*

24 Wherefore now we do declare unto thee, O lord the king, that if this city be built *again*, and the walls thereof set up anew, thou shalt from henceforth have no passage into Celosyria and Phenice.
Precept: Celosyria = *SEE-loh-SIHR-ih-uh; A location. The eastern harbor of Corinth: Acts 18:18 | Romans 16:1 | Phenice = fig-NIGH-sih; A town with a harbor on the southern side Crete: Acts 27:12*

25 Then the king wrote back again to Rathumus the storywriter, to Beeltethmus, to Semellius the scribe, and to the rest that were in commission, and dwellers in Samaria and Syria and Phenice, after this manner;
Precept: Rathumus = *Rehum the chancellor: Ezra 4:8 | Beeltethmus = BEE-el-TETH-muhs | Semellius = sih-MEL-ih-uhs | Phenice = fig-NIGH-sih; A town with a harbor on the southern side Crete: Acts 27:12*

26 I have read the epistle which ye have sent unto me: therefore I

commanded to make diligent search, and it hath been found that that city was from the beginning practising against kings;
Precept: **Epistle** = *Letter*

27 and the men therein *were* given to rebellion and war: and *that* mighty kings and fierce were in Jerusalem, who reigned and exacted tributes in Celosyria and Phenice.
Precept: **Celosyria** = *SEE-loh-SIHR-ih-uh; A location. The eastern harbor of Corinth: Acts 18:18 | Romans 16:1 |* **Phenice** = *fig-NIGH-sih; A town with a harbor on the southern side Crete: Acts 27:12*

28 Now therefore I have commanded to hinder those men from building the city, and heed to be taken that there be no more done in it;

29 and *that those* wicked workers proceed no further to the annoyance of kings,

30 Then king Artexerxes his letters being read, Rathumus, and Semellius the scribe, and the rest that were in commission with them, removing in haste toward Jerusalem with a troop of horsemen and a multitude of people in battle array, began to hinder the builders; and the building of the temple in Jerusalem ceased until the second year of the reign of Darius king of the Persians.
Precept: **Artexerxes** = *ar-TAKS-urk'-sez |* **Rathumus** = *Rehum the chancellor: Ezra 4:8 |* **Semellius** = *sih-MEL-ih-uhs |* **Persians** = *our-SHANZ: Country laying east of Mesopotamia (modern Iraq) |* **Darius** = *duh-RIGH-uhs*

1 ESDRAS CHAPTER 3

1 Now when Darius reigned, he made a great feast unto all his subjects, and unto all his household, and unto all the princes of Media and Persia,
Precept: Darius = duh-RIGH-uhs | 1 Maccabees 12:7

2 and to all the governors and captains and lieutenants that were under him, from India unto Ethiopia, of an hundred twenty and seven provinces.
Precept: Rest of Esther 1:1; 8:9; 9:30; 13:1

3 And when they had eaten and drunken, and being satisfied were gone home, then Darius the king went into his bedchamber, and slept, and *soon after* awaked.
Precept: Darius = duh-RIGH-uhs

4 Then three young men, that were of the guard that kept the king's body, spake one to another;

5 Let every one of us speak a sentence: he that shall overcome, and whose sentence shall seem wiser than the others, unto him shall the king Darius give great gifts, and great things in token of victory:
Precept: Darius = duh-RIGH-uhs

6 as, to be clothed in purple, to drink in gold, and to sleep upon gold, and a chariot with bridles of gold, and an headtire of fine linen, and a chain about his neck:

7 and he shall sit next to Darius because of his wisdom, and shall be called Darius his cousin.
Precept: Darius = duh-RIGH-uhs

8 And then every one wrote his sentence, sealed *it*, and laid *it* under king Darius his pillow;
Precept: Darius = duh-RIGH-uhs

9 And said *that*, when the king is risen, *some* will give him the writings; and of whose side the king and the three princes of Persia shall judge that his sentence is the wisest, to him shall the victory be given, as was appointed.
Precept: Persia = *PUHR-zhuh: Country laying east of Mesopotamia (modern Iraq)*

10 The first wrote, Wine is the strongest.

11 The second wrote, The king is strongest.

12 The third wrote, Women are strongest: but above all *things* Truth beareth away the victory.

13 Now when the king was risen up, they took their writings, and delivered *them* unto him, and so he read them:

14 And sending forth he called all the princes of Persia and Media, and the governors, and the captains, and the lieutenants, and the chief officers;
Precept: Persia = *PUHR-zhuh: Country laying east of Mesopotamia (modern Iraq)*

15 and sat him down in the royal seat of judgment; and the writings were read before them.

16 And he said, Call the young men, and they shall declare their own sentences. So they were called, and came in.

17 And he said unto them, Declare unto us your mind concerning the writings. Then began the first, who had spoken of the strength of wine;

18 And he said thus, O *ye* men, how exceeding strong is wine! it causeth all men to err that drink it:

19 it maketh the mind of the king and of the fatherless child *to be*

all one; of the bondman and of the freeman, of the poor *man* and of the rich:

20 it turneth also every thought into jollity and mirth, so that *a man* remembereth neither sorrow nor debt:

21 and it maketh every heart rich, so that *a man* remembereth neither king nor governor; and it maketh to speak all *things* by talents:

22 and when they are in their cups, they forget their love *both* to friends and brethren, and a little after draw out swords:

Precept: Brethren = *breth-ran: means: Referring to the members of a Sect, society, or of Profession. Many times used as Brother: Genesis 9:22, 25; 19:7 | Deuteronomy 3:20; 10:9 | 1 Esdras 8:47 | Tobit 1:3*

23 but when they are from the wine, they remember not what they have done.

24 O *ye* men, is not wine the strongest, that enforceth to do thus? And when he had so spoken, he held his peace.

1 ESDRAS CHAPTER 4

1 Then the second, that had spoken of the strength of the king, began to say,

2 O *ye* men, do not men excel in strength that bear rule over sea and land and all *things* in them?

3 But yet the king is more mighty: for he is lord of all these *things*, and hath dominion over them; and whatsoever he commandeth them they do.

4 If he bid them make war the one against the other, they do *it*: if he send them out against the enemies, they go, and break down mountains walls and towers.

5 They slay and are slain, and transgress not the king's commandment: if they get the victory, they bring all to the king, as well the spoil, as all *things* else.

6 Likewise for those that are no soldiers, and have not to do with wars, but use husbandry, when they have reaped again that which they had sown, they bring *it* to the king, and compel one another to pay tribute unto the king.
Precept: Husbandry = *The ground, the land, (love the land/ground, or cursed): Genesis 2:9; 3:17; 9:20 |*

7 And yet he is but one *man*: if he command to kill, they kill; if he command to spare, they spare;

8 *if* he command to smite, they smite; *if* he command to make desolate, they make desolate; *if* he command to build, they build;

9 *If* he command to cut down, they cut down; *if* he command to plant, they plant.

10 So all his people and his armies obey him: furthermore he lieth down, he eateth and drinketh, and taketh his rest:

11 and these keep *watch* round about him, neither may any one depart, and do his own business, neither disobey they him in *any thing*.

12 O *ye* men, how should not the king be mightiest, when in such sort he is obeyed? And he held his tongue.

13 Then the third, who had spoken of women, and *of* the truth, (this was Zorobabel) began to speak.
*Precept: **Zorobabel** = zoo-RAHB-uh-buhl, or Zerubbabel = zuh-RUHB-uh-buhl; means: Desendant of Babel*

14 O *ye* men, it is not the great king, nor the multitude of men, neither is it wine, that excelleth; who is it then that ruleth them, or hath the lordship over them? are they not women?

15 Women have borne the king and all the people that bear rule by sea and land.

16 Even of them came they: and they nourished them up that planted the vineyards, from whence the wine cometh.

17 These also make garments for men; these bring glory unto men; and without women cannot men be.

18 Yea, and if *men* have gathered together gold and silver, or any other goodly thing, do they not love a woman *which is* comely in favour and beauty?

19 And letting all those *things* go, do they not gape, and even with open mouth fix their eyes fast on her; and have not all *men* more desire unto her than unto silver or gold, or any goodly thing whatsoever?

20 A man leaveth his own father that brought him up, and his own country, and cleaveth unto his wife.

21 He sticketh not to spend his life with his wife. and remembereth neither father, nor mother, nor country.

22 By this also ye must know that women have dominion over you: do ye not labour and toil, and give and bring all to the woman?

23 Yea, a man taketh his sword, and goeth his way to rob and to steal, to sail upon the sea and *upon* rivers;

24 and looketh upon a lion, and goeth in the darkness; and when he hath stolen, spoiled, and robbed, he bringeth *it* to his love.

25 Wherefore a man loveth his wife better than father or mother.

26 Yea, many there be that have run out of their wits for women, and become servants for their sakes.

27 Many also have perished, have erred, and sinned, for women.

28 And now do ye not believe me? is not the king great in his power? do not all regions fear to touch him?

29 Yet did I see him and Apame the king's concubine, the daughter of the admirable Bartacus, sitting at the right hand of the king,

Precept: Apame = *uh-PAY-mee; means: Dominated. She dominated the king, sitting at the right hand* | **Bartacus** = *BAHR-tuh-kuhs; means: The Illustrious*

30 And taking the crown from the king's head, and setting *it* upon her own head; she also struck the king with *her* left hand.

31 And *yet* for all this the king gaped and gazed upon her with open mouth: if she laughed upon him, he laughed *also*: but if she took any displeasure at him, *the king* was fain to flatter, that she might be reconciled to him *again*.

32 O *ye* men, how can it be but women *should be* strong, seeing they do thus?

33 Then the king and the princes looked one upon another: so he began to speak of the truth.

34 O *ye* men, *are* not women strong? great is the earth, high *is* the heaven, swift *is* the sun in *his* course, for he compasseth the heavens round about, and fetcheth his course again to his own place in one day.
*Precept: **Heaven** = Firmament Separated from he earth. The color blue of the sky was attributed to the chaotic waters that the firmament is separated: Genesis 1:7 | Deuteronomy 5:8 | Job 26:11 | 2 Samuel 22:8*

35 *Is* he not great that maketh these *things?* therefore great is the truth, and stronger than all *things*.

36 All the earth crieth upon the truth, and the heaven blesseth it: all works shake and tremble at it, and with it is no unrighteous *thing*.
*Precept: **Heaven** = Firmament Separated from he earth. The color blue of the sky was attributed to the chaotic waters that the firmament is separated: Genesis 1:7 | Deuteronomy 5:8 | Job 26:11 | 2 Samuel 22:8*

37 Wine *is* wicked, the king *is* wicked, women *are* wicked, all the children of men *are* wicked, and such *are* all their wicked works; and there is no truth in them; in their unrighteousness also they shall perish.

38 As for the truth, it endureth, and is always strong; it liveth and conquereth for evermore.

39 With her there is no accepting of persons or rewards; but she doeth the t*hings that are* just, *and* refraineth from all unjust and wicked *things*; and all *men* do well like of her works.

40 Neither in her judgment is any unrighteousness; and she is the strength, kingdom, power, and majesty, of all ages. Blessed *be* the God of truth.
*Precept: **Blessed*** = *Knowledge of God, All things, Giving knowledge of, Works, The Heavenly Gift of Knowledge, give understanding and knowledge of Blessed = Hallowed, Joined to, Joined, Give, Joined together, Gave knowledge to, Commanded , Praised, Holy, Render, Named Bless = Worship, Give, will Give, Will give you, give us a, praise, Nehemiah 9:5 | Genesis 1:22 | Psalm 33:12 | 2 Esdras 13:24 | **Unrighteousness** = Sin, Wickedness, Injustice, violation of the divine law of God, Ungodly acts, Abomination(s), Fools building upon sand: Matthew 7:26 | Exodus 23:1 | Leviticus 19:15 | Deuteronomy 25:16 | Tobit 4:5; 12:8 | Wisdom 1:5 | Sirach/ Ecclesiasticus 7:3; 17:14*

41 And *with that* he held his peace. And all the people then shouted, and said, Great is Truth, and mighty above all things.

42 Then said the king unto him, Ask what thou wilt more than is appointed in the writing, and we will give *it* thee, because thou art found wisest; and thou shalt sit next me, and shalt be called my cousin.

43 Then said he unto the king, Remember thy vow, which thou hast vowed to build Jerusalem, in the day when thou camest to thy kingdom,

44 And to send away all the vessels that were taken *away* out of Jerusalem, which Cyrus set apart, when he vowed to destroy Babylon, and to send them again thither.
*Precept: **Babylon** = Confuse, Confound; An enormously important city in antiquity ("gate of the god") | **Cyrus** = SIGH-ruhs*

45 Thou also hast vowed to build *up* the temple, which the Edomites burned when Judea was made desolate by the Chaldees.
*Precept: 2 Chronicles 21:8-9; 21:10; 28:17 | **Judea** = The country of Jewry, County of*

the Jews: Ezra 5:8 | 1 Esdras 1:26; 2:5, 12 | Tobit 1:18 | Judith 1:12 | 1 Maccabees 4:35 | Matthew 2:5 | **Chaldees** *= Chaldeans*

46 And now, O lord the king, this is *that* which I require, and which I desire of thee, and this is the princely liberality proceeding from thyself: I desire therefore that thou make good the vow, the performance whereof with thine own mouth thou hast vowed to the King of heaven.
Precept: **Heaven** *= Firmament Separated from he earth. The color blue of the sky was attributed to the chaotic waters that the firmament is separated: Genesis 1:7 | Deuteronomy 5:8 | Job 26:11 | 2 Samuel 22:8*

47 Then Darius the king stood up, and kissed him, and wrote letters for him unto all the treasurers and lieutenants and captains and governors, that they should safely convey on their way *both* him, and all those that go up with him to build Jerusalem.
Precept: **Darius** *= duh-RIGH-uhs*

48 He wrote letters also unto the lieutenants that were in Celosyria and Phenice, and unto them in Libanus, that *they* should bring cedar wood from Libanus unto Jerusalem, and that they should build the city with him.
Precept: **Celosyria** *= SEE-loh-SIHR-ih-uh; A location. The eastern harbor of Corinth: Acts 18:18 | Romans 16:1 |* **Phenice** *= fig-NIGH-sih; A town with a harbor on the southern side Crete: Acts 27:12 |* **Libanus** *is another form of saying* **Lebanon***; means: To be white, or The white mountain of Syria (White meaning snow): Jeremiah 18:14*

49 Moreover he wrote for all the Jews that went out of *his* realm up into Jewry, concerning their freedom, that no officer, no ruler, no lieutenant, nor treasurer, should forcibly enter into their doors;
Precept: **Jewry** *= The country of Judea, Judah: Daniel 5:13 | Luke 23:5 | John 7:1*

50 and that all the country which they hold should be free without tribute; and that the Edomites should give over the villages of the Jews which *then* they held:
Precept: 2 Chronicles 28:17

51 yea, that there should be yearly given twenty talents to the building of the temple, until the time that it were built;

52 and other ten talents yearly, to maintain the burnt offerings upon the altar every day, as they had a commandment to offer seventeen:

53 and that all they that went from Babylon to build the city should have free liberty, as well they as their posterity, and all the priests that went *away*.
Precept: Babylon = *Confuse, Confound; An enormously important city in antiquity ("gate of the god") | Priests = Called Ministers*

54 He wrote also concerning. the charges, and the priests' vestments wherein they minister;
Precept: Priests = *Called Ministers*

55 and likewise for the charges of the Levites, to be given *them* until the day that the house were finished, and Jerusalem builded *up*.

56 And he commanded to give to all that kept the city pensions and wages.

57 He sent away also all the vessels from Babylon, that Cyrus had set apart; and all that Cyrus had given in commandment, *the same* charged he also to be done, and sent unto Jerusalem.
Precept: Babylon = *Confuse, Confound; An enormously important city in antiquity ("gate of the god") | Cyrus = SIGH-ruhs*

58 Now when *this* young man was gone forth, he lifted up *his* face to heaven toward Jerusalem, and praised the King of heaven,
Precept: Heaven = *Firmament Separated from he earth. The color blue of the sky was attributed to the chaotic waters that the firmament is separated: Genesis 1:7 | Deuteronomy 5:8 | Job 26:11 | 2 Samuel 22:8*

59 and said, From thee *cometh* victory, from thee *cometh* wisdom, and thine *is* the glory, and I am thy servant.

60 Blessed art thou, who hast given me wisdom: for to thee I give thanks, O Lord of *our* fathers.

Precept: Blessed = *Knowledge of God, All things, Giving knowledge of, Works, The Heavenly Gift of Knowledge, give understanding and knowledge of Blessed = Hallowed, Joined to, Joined, Give, Joined together, Gave knowledge to, Commanded , Praised, Holy, Render, Named Bless = Worship, Give, will Give, Will give you, give us a, praise, Nehemiah 9:5 | Genesis 1:22 | Psalm 33:12 | 2 Esdras 13:24*

61 And *so* he took the letters, and went out, and came unto Babylon, and told *it* all his brethren.

Precept: Babylon = *Confuse, Confound; An enormously important city in antiquity ("gate of the god") | Brethren = breth-ran: means: Referring to the members of a Sect, society, or of Profession. Many times used as Brother: Genesis 9:22, 25; 19:7 | Deuteronomy 3:20; 10:9 | 1 Esdras 8:47 | Tobit 1:3*

62 And they praised the God of their fathers, because he had given them freedom and liberty

63 to go up, and to build Jerusalem, and the temple which is called by his name: and they feasted with *instruments* of musick and gladness seven days.

1 ESDRAS CHAPTER 5

1 After this were the principal men of the families chosen according to their tribes, to go up with their wives and sons and daughters, with their menservants and maidservants, and their cattle.

2 And Darius sent with them a thousand horsemen, till they had brought them back to Jerusalem safely, and with musical *instruments* tabrets and flutes.
Precept: Darius = *duh-RIGH-uhs*

3 And all their brethren played, and he made them go up together with them.
Precept: Brethren = *breth-ran: means: Referring to the members of a Sect, society, or of Profession. Many times used as Brother: Genesis 9:22, 25; 19:7 | Deuteronomy 3:20; 10:9 | 1 Esdras 8:47 | Tobit 1:3*

4 And these *are* the names of the men which went up, according to their families among their tribes, after their several heads.

5 The priests, the sons of Phinees the son of Aaron: Jesus the son of Josedec, the son of Saraias, and Joacim the son of Zorobabel, the son of Salathiel, of the house of David, out of the kindred of Phares, of the tribe of Judah;
Precept: Joacim = *JOH-uh-kim* | **Phinees** = *Fin-ih-uhs is Greek. His Hebrew name is* **Phinehas** = *FIN-ih-huhs; means: Dark-skinned one. One of Ezra's progenitors: 2 Esdras 1:2. However, this link is not found in Ezra's genealogy checking 1 Esdras 8:1, Ezra 7:1, or 1 Chronicles chapter 6. this will be found in 2 Esdras 1:2, Ezra's descent was from Eleazar, while Phinees (Phinehas) was a direct descendant of Ithamar, the youngest son of Aaron.* | **Josedec** = *JAHS-uh-dek, or* **Jozadak** = *JAHZ-uh-dak; means: Yahawah acts in righteousness: 1 Chronicles 6:14-15 | Haggai 1:1 | Ezra 3:2* | **Saraias** = *such-RAY-yuhs; means: Yahawah has persevered or persisted* | **Joacim** = *JOH-uh-kim, or* **Joacim** = *JOH-uh-kim* | **Zorobabel** = *zoo-RAHB-uh-buhl, or* **Zerubbabel** = *zuh-RUHB-uh-buhl; means: Desendant of Babel* | **Salathiel** = *suh-LAY-thih-el; means: I have asked of Yahawah/God: 1 Chronicles 3:17* | **Phares** = *FEHR-iss, is the Greek name . The Hebrew name is Pharez* = *FEHR-iz; means: Breach* | **David** = *DAY-vid. The name David is a suggested title to the throne, not a personal name; means: The True Messiah*

6 Who spake wise sentences before Darius the king of Persia in the second year of his reign, in the month Nisan, *which is* the first month.

*Precept: **Darius** = duh-RIGH-uhs | **Persia** = PUHR-zhuh: Country laying east of Mesopotamia (modern Iraq)*

7 And these are they of Jewry that came up from the captivity, where they dwelt as strangers, whom Nabuchodonosor the king of Babylon had carried away unto Babylon.

*Precept: **Babylon** = Confuse, Confound; An enormously important city in antiquity ("gate of the god") | **Nabuchodonosor** = NAB-uh-kuh-DAHN-ub-sawr*

8 And they returned unto Jerusalem, and to the other parts of Jewry, every man to his own city, who came with Zorobabel, with Jesus, Nehemias, *and* Zacharias, *and* Resaias, Enenius, Mardocheus. Beelsarus, Aspharasus, Reelius, Roimus, *and* Baana, their guides.

*Precept: **Zacharias** = ZAK-uh-RIGH-uhs; means: Yahweh remembers | **Jewry** = The country of Judea, Judah: Daniel 5:13 | Luke 23:5 | John 7:1 | **Zorobabel** = zoo-RAHB-uh-buhl, or **Zerubbabel** = zuh-RUHB-uh-buhl; means: Descendant of Babel | **Nehemias** = NEE-huh-MIGH-uhs, **Nehemiah** = NEE-huh-MIGH-uh; means: Yahawah comforts, encourages: Ezra 2:2 | Nehemiah 7:7 | **Zacharias** = ZAK-uh-RIGH-uhs; means: Yahweh remembers | **Resaias** is **Resaiah** = REE-el-IGH-uh; means: Yahawah has caused trembling| **Enenius** is the same person named **Bigvai** = BIG-vay-igh; means: god, or fortune: Ezra 2:2 | Nehemiah 7:7 | **Mardocheus** = MAHR-duh-KEE-uhs; means: Gentile: the same person **Mordecai**:Esther 2:5 | Ezra 2:2 | **Beelsarus** = bee-ELL-suh-ruhs, is the same person named **Bilshan** = BiL-shan; means: Their lord: Ezra 2:2 | Nehemiah 7:7 | **Aspharasus** = ass-FEHR-uh-suhs, is the same person named **Mispar** = MISS-pahr; means: Writing: Ezra 2:2 | Nehemiah 7:7 | **Reelius** = REE-uh-LIGH-uhs, is the same person named **Reelaiah** = REE-el-IGH-uh: Ezra 2:2 | Nehemiah 7:7 | **Roimus** = ROH-ih-muhs, is the same person named **Rehum** = REE-huhm; means; Merciful: Ezra 2:2 | Nehemiah 7:7 | **Baana** = BAY-uh-nuh; means: soon oppression*

9 The number of them of the nation, and their governors, sons of Phoros, two thousand an hundred seventy and two; the sons of Saphat, four hundred seventy and two:

*Precept: **Phoros** = FAHR-ahs, is the same person named **Parosh** = PAY-rahsh: means: Flea | **Saphat** = SAY-fat*

10 the sons of Ares, seven hundred fifty and six:

*Precept: **Ares** = EHR-eez*

11 the sons of Phaath Moab, two thousand eight hundred and twelve:
Precept: Phaath Moab = PAY-hath-MOH-ab; means: Governor of Moab, also found under the name Eliehoenai: Ezra 8:4 | 1 Esdras 8:31

12 the sons of Elam, a thousand two hundred fifty and four: the sons of Zathui, nine hundred forty and five: the sons of Corbe, seven hundred and five: the sons of Bani, six hundred forty and eight:
Precept: Elam = EE-luhm; means Highland | Zathui = ZATG-oo-ee, Zattu = ZAT-oo, is the same person: Ezra 2:8; 10:27 | Nehemiah 7:13 | Corbe = KAWR-bee | Bani = BAY-nigh; means: Built

13 the sons of Bebai, six hundred twenty and three: the sons of Sadas, three thousand two hundred twenty and two:
Precept: Bebai = BEE-bigh; means: Child | Sadas = SAY-duhs

14 the sons of Adonikam, six hundred sixty and seven: the sons of Bagoi, two thousand sixty and six: the sons of Adin, four hundred fifty and four:
Precept: Adonikam = ad-oh-NIGH-kuhm; means: the Lord has arisen: Ezra 2:13; 8:13 | Nehemiah 7:18 | Bagoi = BAY-goy | Adin = AY-din; means Luxury, Deligh

15 the sons of Aterezias, ninety and two: the sons of Ceilan and Azetas threescore and seven: the sons of Azuran, four hundred thirty and two:
Precept: Aterezias = uh-tehr-uh-ZIGH-uhs; means: The Ater of Hezekiah | Ceilan = SEE-luhn | Azetas = uh-ZEE-tuhs | Azuran = uh-ZOO-ruhn, Azaru = an-uh-NIGH-uhs

16 the sons of Ananias, an hundred and one: the sons of Arom, thirty two: and the sons of Bassa, three hundred twenty and three: the sons of Azephurith, an hundred and two:
Precept: Ananias = uh-tehr-uh-ZIGH-uhs; means: Yahawah has dealt graciously | Bassa = BAS-saw, Bezai is the same person; means: To shine | Aron = EHR-uhm | Azephurith = uh-ZEF-uh-rith

17 the sons of Meterus, three thousand and five: the sons of

34

Bethlomon, an hundred twenty and three:
Precept: Meterus = *muh-TEE-ruhs* | ***Bethlomon*** = *beth-LO-mon*

18 They of Netophah, fifty and five: they of Anathoth, an hundred fifty and eight: they of Bethsamos, forty and two:
Precept: Netophah = *nih-TOH-fuh* | ***Anathoth*** = *AN-uh-thawth* | ***Bethsamos*** = *beth-SAM-ahs*

19 they of Kiriathiarius, twenty and five: they of Caphira and Beroth, seven hundred forty and three: they of Pira, seven hundred:
Precept: Kiriathiarius = *KIHR-ih-ath-ih-EHR-ih-uhs* | ***Caphira*** = *kuh-FIGH-rim* | ***Beroth*** = *BIHR-ahth* | ***Pira*** = *PIGH-ruh*

20 they of Chadias and Ammidoi, four hundred twenty and two: they of Cirama and Gabdes, six hundred twenty and one:
Precept: Chadias = *KAY-dih-uhs* | ***Ammidoi*** = *AM-uh-doy* | ***Gabdes*** = *GAB-deez*

21 they of Macalon, an hundred twenty and two: they of Betolius, fifty and two: the sons of Nephis, an hundred fifty and six:
Precept: Macalon = *muh-KAL-ahn, is the Greek name. I Herbew the name is* ***Michmas*** = *muh-KAL-ahn: Ezra 2:27* | *Nehemiah 7:31* | ***Nephis*** = *NEF-igh, in Greek. In Hebrew the name is* ***Magbish*** = *MAG-bish; means: Pile* | ***Betolius*** = *bih-TOH-lih-uhs*

22 the sons of Calamolalus and Onus, seven hundred twenty and five: the sons of Jerechus, two hundred forty and five:
Precept: Calamolalus = *KAL-uh-MAHL-uh-luhs* | ***Onus*** = *OH-nuhs* | ***Jerechus*** = *JEHR-uh-kuhs*

23 the sons of Annas, three thousand three hundred and thirty.
Precept: Annas = *AN-uhs; means: Merciful*

24 The priests: the sons of Jeddu, the son of Jesus among the sons of Sanasib, nine hundred seventy and two: the sons of Meruth, a thousand fifty and two:
Precept: Jeddu = *JED-oo, in Greek. In Hebrew his name is* ***Jedaiah*** = *Jim-DIGH-uh; means: Yahawah Knows: Ezra 2:36 and Nehemiah 7:39* | ***Sanasib*** = *SAN-uh-sib*

25 the sons of Phassaron, a thousand forty and seven: the sons of Carme, a thousand and seventeen.

Precept: Phassaron = *FASS-uh-rahn, in Greek. In Hebrew his name is* **Pashhur**, *or* **Pashur** = *PASH-huhr: Ezra 2:38 | Nehemiah 7:41 | 1 Chronicles 9:12 | Ezra 10:22 |* **Carme** = *KAHR-mee, is the Greek meaning. His Hebrew name is* **Harim** = *HAY-rim; means: dedicated, Flat-nose: 1 Chronicles 24:8 | Ezra 2:32 | Nehemiah 10:5, 27*

26 the Levites: the sons of Jessue, and Cadmiel, and Bannas, and Sudias, seventy and four.

Precept: Jessue = *JESH-yoo-ee. Same as Jesus |* **Cadmiel** = *KAD-mih-uhl is the Greek name. His Hebrew name is* **Kadmiel** = *KAD-mih-el; means: God is of old: Ezra 2:40 | Nehemiah 7:43; 12:8 |* **Bannas** = *BAN-nass |* **Sudias** = *SoO-dih-uhs, is the Greek name. His Hebrew name is* **Hodaviah/Hodevah** = *HOH-dih-vah; Praise Yahawah*

27 The holy singers: the sons of Asaph, an hundred twenty and eight.

Precept: Asaph = *AY-saf; means: He collected*

28 The porters: the sons of Salum, the sons of Jatal, the sons of Talmon, the sons of Dacobi, the sons of Teta, the sons of Sami, in all an hundred thirty and nine.

Precept: Salum = *SAY-luhm, and* **Shallum** = *SHAL-uhm; means: Replacer: Ezra Ezra 7:2 |* **Jatal** = *JAY-tuhl is Greek. His Hebrew name is* **Ater** = *AY-tuhr; means: Crippled, or Left-handed: Ezra 2:16 | Nehemiah 7:21, 10:18 |* **Talmon** = *TAL-mahn; means: Brightness. Parallels: Ezra 4:42 | 1 Chronicles 9:17 | Nehemiah 11:19; 7:45 |* **Dacobi** = *Day-kuh-bigh is Greek. His Hebrew name is* **Akkub** = *AK-uhb; means Protector, protector one, some called "The Gatekeeper": 1 Chronicles 9:17 | Ezra 2:42 | Nehemiah 7:45; 11:19; 12:25 |* **Teta** = *TAY-tuh is Greek. The Hebrew name is* **Hatita** = *huh-TIGH-tuh; means: bored a hole, soft: Ezra 2:42 | Nehemiah 7:45 |* **Sami** = *SAY-migh is Greek. His Hebrew name is* **Shobai** = *SHOH-bay-igh: Ezra 2:42 | Nehemiah 7:45. The different version of the Apocrypha use three transliterations of this word: Sobai, Sabei, and Tobbis. These differences do not appear, however, in the English versions.*

29 The servants of the temple: the sons of Esau, the sons of Asipha, the sons of Tabaoth, the sons of Ceras, the sons of Sud, the sons of Phaleas, the sons of Labana, the sons of Graba,

Precept: Esau = *EE-saw; means: Hairy |* **Asipha** = *uh-SIF-uh is Greek. His name in Hebrew is* **Hasupha** = *huh-SOO-fuh; means: Quick: Ezra 2:43 | Nehemiah 7:46 |* **Tabaoth** = *TA-ba-ohth, also* **Tabbath** = *TAB-ay-ahth in Hebrew; means: Signet rings: Ezra 2:43 | Nehemiah 7:46 |* **Ceras** = *SER-ras, is Greek. In Hebrew his name is* **Keros**

= KEE-rahs; means: Bent: Ezra 2:44 | Nehemiah 7:47 | **Sud** = SUHD; means: My secret, Ensnaring, hunting: Proverbs 6:26 | Micah 7:2 | **Phaleas** = fun-LEE-uhs is Greek. In Hebrew his name is **Padon** = PAY-dahn; means: Redemption. Parallel Ezra 2:44, and Nehemiah 7:4 7 | **Labana** = luh-BAY-nuh is Greek. In Hebrew his name is **Lebana** = lib-BAY-nuh; means: White, full. The name appears in Ezra 2:45 in the phrase "the sons of **Lebanah**. In parallel passages in Nehemiah 7:46-56 he's lists "the sons of **Lebana**" in Nehemiah 7:48 | **Graba** = GRAH-buh is Greek. His name in Hebrew is **Hagabah** = HAG-uh-buh; means: Locust: Ezra 2:45 | Nehemiah 7:48

30 the sons of Acua, the sons of Uta, the sons of Cetab, the sons of Agaba, the sons of Subai, the sons of Anan, the sons of Cathua, the sons of Geddur,

Precept: Acua = uh-KYOO-uh is Greek. His name in Hebrew is **Akkub** = AK-uhb; means: Pursuer: Ezra 2:42 | Nehemiah 7:45 | **Uta** = UTA is Greek. His name in Hebrew is **Uthai** = YOO-thigh; means one of many: My helper, Yahawah is help, and He has shown himself supreme: Ezra 8:14 | 1 Chronicles 9:4 | **Cetab** = SEE-tab is greek. His name in Hebrew is **Ketab** = KEE-tab; means; denoting an "edict" | **Agaba** = AG-uh-huh, is Greek. His name in Hebrew is **Hagabah** = HAG-un-buh; means: Grasshopper; leaper; a locust. Name sometimes used as **Hagaba**: Nehemiah 7:48 | Ezra 2:45 | **Subai** = SOO-bigh is Greek. His name in Hebrew is **Shalmai** = SHAL-migh; means: Coat: Ezra 2:46 | Nehemiah 7:48 | **Anan** = AY-nan; means: A cloud, He beclouds of covers, Cloud. In Ezra 2:46 he is called **Hanan** = HAY-nan; means: Yahawah is gracious: Ezra 2:46 | 1 Chronicles 8:23 | **Cathua** = huh-THOO-uh. He is called in Ezra 2:47 "**Giddel**" = GID-uhl; means: He made great, Praised, and Very great: Ezra 2:56 | **Geddur** = GED-uhr, or **Gahar** = GAY-hahr; means: Drought, small in spirit: Ezra 2:47 | Nehemiah 7:49

31 the sons of Airus, the sons of Daisan, the sons of Noeba, the sons of Chaseba, the sons of Gazera, the sons of Azia, the sons of Phinees, the sons of Azara, the sons of Bastai, the sons of Asana, the sons of Meani, the sons of Naphisi, the sons of Acub, the sons of Acipha, the sons of Assur, the sons of Pharacim, the sons of Basaloth,

Precept: Airus = AY-ruhs is Greek. His Hebrew name is **Jairus, or Jair** = JIGH-ruhs; means Yahawah will enlighten, He enlightens: Numbers 32:41 | Deuteronomy 3:14 Joshua 13:30 | Mark 5:22 | **Daisan** = DAY-suhn, another translation is **Rezin** = REE-zin; means: Pleasant, agreeable: 2 Kings 15:37 | **Noeba** = now-EE-huh is Greek. His Hebrew name is **Nekoda** = nih-KOH-duh; means: speckled, Spotted: Ezra 2:48 | Nehemiah 7:50 | **Chaseba** = KASS-uh-buh, is Greek. He has two spellings of his name in Hebrew his name is 1. **Achzib** = AK-zib; means: Deceitful: Joshua 15:44 | Micah 1:14. 2. **Chezib** = KEE-zib; means: Lying, Deceptive, False: Genesis 38:5 | **Gazera** = ugh-ZEE-ruh is Greek. His Hebrew name is **Gazzam** = GAZ-uhm; means: Caterpillar, or Bird of prey: Ezra 2:48 | **Azia** = AZ-ih-uh, is Greek. His Hebrew name is **Uzza** = UHZ-uh; means Yahawah/El (God) is my Strength | **Phinees** = Fin-ih-uhs is Greek. His Hebrew name is **Phinehas** = FIN-ih-huhs; means: Dark-skinned one. One of

*Ezra's progenitors: 2 Esdras 1:2. However, this link is not found in Ezra's genealogy checking 1 Esdras 8:1, Ezra 7:1, or 1 Chronicles chapter 6. this will be found in 2 Esdras 1:2, Ezra's descent was from Eleazar, while Phinees (Phinehas) was a direct descendant of Ithamar, the youngest son of Aaron | **Azara** = AZ-uh-ruh, is Greek. His Hebrew **Hasrah** = HAZ-ruh: 2 Kings 22:14 | **Bastai** = BASS-tigh, is Greek. His name in Hebrew is **Besai** = BEE-sigh; meaning: downtrodden: Nehemiah 7:52 | Ezra 2:49 | **Asana** = uh-SAH-nuh, is Greek. His name in **Asnah** = ASS-nuh; means: Thornbush: Ezra 2:50 | **Meani** = mid-AY-nigh, is Greek. His name in Hebrew **Meunim** = mih-YOO-nim: Ezra 2:50 | Nehemiah 7:52 | **Naphisi** = NAF-ih-sigh, is Hebrew name is **Naphish** = NAY-fish; means: Refreshed: Genesis 25:15 | **Acub** = AY-kuhb, is Greek. In Hebrew his name is **Akkub** = AK-uhb; means: Protector, Protector One | **Acipha** = uh-SIGH-fuh, is Greek. In Hebrew is **Hakupha**; means: Bent: Ezra 2:51 | Nehemiah 7:53 | **Assur** = ASH-uhr: Ezra 4:2 | Psalm 83:8 | **Basaloth** = BASS-uh-lahth, his name in Hebrew is **Bazlith** = BAZ-lith; means: In the shadow, or Onions: Nehemiah 7:54*

32 the sons of Meeda, the sons of Coutha, the sons of Charea, the sons of Charcus, the sons of Aserer, the sons of Thomoi, the sons of Nasith, the sons of Atipha.

Precept: Meeda = meh-EE-duh, is Greek. In Hebrew, his name is **Mehida** = meh-HIGH-duh; means: Brought, Renowned: Ezra 2:52 | Nehemiah 7:54 | **Coutha** = KOO-thuh, is Greek. **Cutha** = KYOO-thuh: Ezra 2:52 | Nehemiah 7:54 | **Charea** = KEHR-ee-uh, is Greek. His Hebrew name is **Harsha** = HAHR-shuh; means: Unable to talk, Slient, Magician, or Sorcerer: Ezra 2:52 | Nehemiah 7:54 | **Charcus** = KAHR-kuhs, is Greek, he has an Aramaic name: **Barkos** = BAHR-kahs; means: A god: Ezra 2:53 | Nehemiah 7:55 | **Aserer** = AY-suh-ruhr, is Greek. His Hebrew translation is **Sisera** = SIS-uh-ruh; means: Servant of Ra: Judges 4:2 | **Thomoi** = THAHM-oy, is Greek. His translated name is **Temah/Thamah** = THAY-muh; means; You will be fat: Ezra 2:53, and the parallel verse: Nehemiah 7:55 | **Nasith** = NAY-sith, is Greek. His translated name is **Neziah** = nit-ZIGH-uh: Ezra 2:54, and the parallel verse: Nehemiah 7:56 | **Atipha** = uh-TIGH-fuh, is Greek. His translated Hebrew name is **Hatipha** = huh-TIGH-fuh; means: Taken, captive: Ezra 2:54 | Nehemiah 7:56

33 The sons of the servants of Solomon: the sons of Azaphion, the sons of Pharira, the sons of Jeeli, the sons of Lozon, the sons of Israel, the sons of Sapheth,

Precept: Solomon = SAHL-uh-muhn; means: Will give Shalom, The LORD's beloved | **Azaphion** = uh-ZAY-fee-uhn, is Greek. The translated name is **Sophereth** = SAHF-uh-reth (the female scribe): Ezra 2:55 | Nehemiah 7:57 | **Pharira** = FA-ri-ra, is Greek. The translated name for Hebrew is **Perida**, or **Peruda** = pih-ROO-duh; means: To separates oneself: Ezra 2:55 | Nehemiah 7:57 | **Jeeli** = JEE-uh-ligh, is Greek. The Hebrew translation is **Jaala/Jaalah** = JAY-uh-luh; means: Mountain goat: Nehemiah 7:58 | Ezra 2:56 | **Lozon** = LOH-zahn, is Greek. The Hebrew translation is **Darkon** = DAHR-kahn; means: Hard: Ezra 2:56 | Nehemiah 7:58 | **Sapheth** = SAY-feth, is Greek. The translation is **Shephatiah** = shef-uh-TIGH-uh; means: The LORD has judged: Ezra 2:57 | Nehemiah 7:59 | **Israel** = IZ-ray-el; means: A prince of God

34 the sons of Hagia, the sons of Phacareth, the sons of Sabi, the sons of Sarothie, the sons of Masias, the sons of Gar, the sons of Addus, the sons of Suba, the sons of Apherra, the sons of Barodis, the sons of Sabat, the sons of Allom.

Precept: Hagia = HAY-ghee-uh, is Greek. The Hebrew translation is Hattil = HAT-ihl: Ezra 2:57 | Nehemiah 7:59 | Phacareth = FAK-uh-reth, is Greek. The Hebrew translation is Pochereth-Hazzebaim = POK-uh-reth-haz-uh-BA-em ; means: Snaring the Antelopes, or Hunter: Ezra 2:57 | Nehemiah 7:59 | Sabi = SA-bi-as | Sarothie = suh-ROH-thee, is Greek | Masias = muh-SIGH-uhs, is Greek | Gar = GAHR, is Greek | Addus = AD-uhs, is Greek. And was also called Jaddus. The Hebrew translation is Barzillai = bahr-ZIL-igh; means: made of iron; Ezra 2:61 | Suba = SOO-buh, is Greek | Apherra = uh-FEHr-un, is Greek | Barodis = buh-ROH-diss, is Greek | Sabat = SAB-uht, is Greek. It derives from the name Shaphat = SHAY-fat; means: to judge: Numbers 13:5 | Allom = AL-ahm; means: Oak

35 All the ministers of the temple, and the sons of the servants of Solomon, were three hundred seventy and two.

Precept: Solomon = SAHL-uh-muhn; means: Will give Shalom, The LORD's beloved | Ministers = Called Priests: Joel 1:9, 13 | Numbers 3:3 | Ezra 8:17 | Psalm 103:21

36 These came up from Thermeleth and Thelersas, Charaathalar leading them, and Aalar;

Precept: Thermeleth = thuhr-MEE-leth, is Greek. The Hebrew translation Tel-melah = tel-MEE-luh; means: The ruined mound of salt: Ezra 2:59 | Nehemiah 7:61 | Thelersas = thih-LUHR-suhs, is Greek. The Hebrew translation is Tel-harsa = tel-HAHR-suh | Charaathalar = kehr-ay-ATH-uh-lahr, is Greek. The Hebrew translation is Cherub = KEHR-uhb; means: Cherubim; Genesis 3:24 | Aalar = AY-uh-luhr, is Greek. The translation is Immer = IM-uhr; means: Lamb: Ezra 2:59 | Nehemiah 3:29

37 neither could they shew their families, nor *their* stock, how they were of Israel: the sons of Ladan, the son of Ban, the sons of Necodan, six hundred fifty and two.

Precept: Ladan = LAY-duhn | Ban = BAN | Necodan = nah-KOH-dan, is Greek. The Hebrew translation is Nekoda = nih-KOH-duh; means: Speckled, spotted | Israel = IZ-ray-el; means: A prince of God

38 And of the priests that usurped the office of the priesthood, and were not found: the sons of Obdia, the sons of Accoz, the sons of Addus, who married Augia *one* of the daughters of Berzelus, and was named after his name.

Precept: Addus = AD-uhs, is Greek. And was also called Jaddus. The Hebrew translation is Barzillai = bahr-ZIL-igh; means: made of iron; Ezra 2:61 | Obdia =

*ahb-DIGH-uh, is Greek. The Hebrew translation is **Habaiah** = huh-BAY-yuh; means: Withdraw, Hide: Ezra 2:61 | Nehemiah 7:63 | **Accoz** = AK-ahz, is Greek. The Hebrew translation is **Koz/Hakkoz** = KAHZ; means: The thorn: Ezra 2:61 | Nehemiah 3:4 | **Augia** = AW-jee-uh, is Greek | **Berzelus** = buhr-ZEE-luhs, is Greek. **Barzillai** = bahr-ZIL-igh; means: Man of iron: Ezra 2:62 | **Priests** = Called Ministers*

39 And when the description of the kindred of these *men* was sought in the register, and was not found, they were removed from executing the office of the priesthood:

40 For unto them said Nehemias and Atharias, that *they* should not be partakers of the holy *things*, till there arose up an high priest clothed with doctrine and truth.
*Precept: **Nehemias** = NEE-huh-MIGH-uhs, is Greek. The Hebrew translation is Nehemiah = NEE-huh-MIGH-uh; means: Yahawah comforts, encourages: Ezra 2:2 | Nehemiah 7:7 | **Atharias** = ath-RIGH-uhs, is Greek*

41 So of Israel, from them of twelve years old and upward, they were all in number forty thousand, beside menservants and womenservants two thousand three hundred and sixty.
*Precept: **Israel** = IZ-ray-el; means: A prince of God*

42 Their menservants and handmaids *were* seven thousand three hundred forty and seven: the singing men and singing *women*, two hundred forty and five:

43 four hundred thirty and five camels, seven thousand thirty and six horses, two hundred forty and five mules, five thousand five hundred twenty and five beasts used to the yoke.

44 And *certain* of the chief of their families, when they came to the temple of God that is in Jerusalem, vowed to set up the house *again* in his own place according to their ability,

45 and to give into the holy treasury of the works a thousand pounds of gold, five thousand of silver, and an hundred priestly vestments.

46 And *so* dwelt the priests and the Levites and the people in Jerusalem, and *in* the country, the singers also and the porters; and all Israel in their villages.
Precept: Israel = IZ-ray-el; means: A prince of God | Priests = Called Ministers

47 But when the seventh month was at hand, and when the children of Israel were every man in his own *place*, they came *all* together with one consent into the open place of the first gate which is toward the east.
Precept: Israel = IZ-ray-el; means: A prince of God

48 Then stood up Jesus the *son* of Josedec, and his brethren the priests and Zorobabel the *son* of Salathiel, and his brethren, and made ready the altar of the God of Israel,
Precept: Josedec = JAHS-uh-dek, or Jozadak = JAHZ-uh-dak; means: Yahawah acts in righteousness: 1 Chronicles 6:14-15 | Haggai 1:1 | Ezra 3:2 | Zorobabel = zoo-RAHB-uh-buhl, or Zerubbabel = zuh-RUHB-uh-buhl; means: Desendant of Babel | Salathiel = such-LAY-thih-el; means: I have asked of Yahawah/God: 1 Chronicles 3:17 | Israel = IZ-ray-el; means: A prince of God | Priests = Called Ministers | Brethren = breth-ran: means: Referring to the members of a Sect, society, or of Profession. Many times used as Brother: Genesis 9:22, 25; 19:7 | Deuteronomy 3:20; 10:9 | 1 Esdras 8:47 | Tobit 1:3

49 to offer burnt sacrifices upon it, according as it is expressly commanded in the book of Moses the man of God.
Precept: Sacrifice = Prepare; Practice: Genesis 27:17 | Exodus 12:39; 15:2; 23:20 | Numbers 15:5-6; 23:1, 29 | Joshua 1:11 | Psalms 103:9 | Proverbs 8:27 | Jonah 4:6-7 | 1 Esdras 1:13-14 | 2 Esdras 8:60; 9:18 | Practice: Sirach/Ecclesiasticus 10:6 | 2 Peter 2:14

50 And there were gathered unto them out of the other nations of the land, and they erected the altar upon his own place, because all the nations of the land were at enmity with them, and oppressed them; and they offered sacrifices according to the time, and burnt offerings to the Lord *both* morning and evening.
Precept: Sacrifice = Prepare; Practice: Genesis 27:17 | Exodus 12:39; 15:2; 23:20 | Numbers 15:5-6; 23:1, 29 | Joshua 1:11 | Psalms 103:9 | Proverbs 8:27 | Jonah 4:6-7 | 1 Esdras 1:13-14 | 2 Esdras 8:60; 9:18 | Practice: Sirach/Ecclesiasticus 10:6 | 2 Peter 2:14

51 Also they held the feast of tabernacles, as it is commanded in the law, and *offered* sacrifices daily, as was meet:
Precept: Sacrifice = *Prepare; Practice: Genesis 27:17 | Exodus 12:39; 15:2; 23:20 | Numbers 15:5-6; 23:1, 29 | Joshua 1:11 | Psalms 103:9 | Proverbs 8:27 | Jonah 4:6-7 | 1 Esdras 1:13-14 | 2 Esdras 8:60; 9:18 | Practice: Sirach/Ecclesiasticus 10:6 | 2 Peter 2:14*

52 and after that, the continual oblations, and the sacrifice of the sabbaths, and of the new moons, and of all holy feasts.
Precept: Sacrifice = *Prepare; Practice: Genesis 27:17 | Exodus 12:39; 15:2; 23:20 | Numbers 15:5-6; 23:1, 29 | Joshua 1:11 | Psalms 103:9 | Proverbs 8:27 | Jonah 4:6-7 | 1 Esdras 1:13-14 | 2 Esdras 8:60; 9:18 | Practice: Sirach/Ecclesiasticus 10:6 | 2 Peter 2:14*

53 And all they that had made *any* vow to God began to offer sacrifices to God from the first day of the seventh month, although the temple of the Lord was not yet built.
Precept: Sacrifice = *Prepare; Practice: Genesis 27:17 | Exodus 12:39; 15:2; 23:20 | Numbers 15:5-6; 23:1, 29 | Joshua 1:11 | Psalms 103:9 | Proverbs 8:27 | Jonah 4:6-7 | 1 Esdras 1:13-14 | 2 Esdras 8:60; 9:18 | Practice: Sirach/Ecclesiasticus 10:6 | 2 Peter 2:14*

54 And they gave unto the masons and carpenters money, meat, and drink, with cheerfulness.

55 Unto them of Zidon also and Tyre they gave carrs, that they should bring cedar trees from Libanus, which should be brought by floats to the haven of Joppe, according as it was commanded them by Cyrus king of the Persians.
Precept: Cyrus = *SIGH-ruhs | **Libanus** is another form of saying **Lebanon**; means: To be white, or The white mountain of Syria (White meaning snow): Jeremiah 18:14 | **Jappe, Japho, or Jappa** = JAHP-uh: A town on the coast of the Mediterranean Sea in connection with the original tribe territory of Dan: Joshua 19:46 | Ezra 3;7 | 2 Chronicles 2:15 | Acts 9:36 | **Persians** = our-SHANZ: Country laying east of Mesopotamia (modern Iraq).*

56 And in the second year *and* second month after his coming to the temple of God at Jerusalem began Zorobabel the son of Salatiel, and Jesus the *son* of Josedec, and their brethren, and the priests, and the Levites, and all they that were come unto

Jerusalem out of the captivity:

Precept: Josedec = *JAHS-uh-dek, or* **Jozadak** = *JAHZ-uh-dak; means: Yahawah acts in righteousness: 1 Chronicles 6:14-15 | Haggai 1:1 | Ezra 3:2 |* **Zorobabel** = *zoo-RAHB-uh-buhl, or* **Zerubbabel** = *zuh-RUHB-uh-buhl; means: Desendant of Babel |* **Salatiel** = *such-LAY-thih-el; means: I have asked of Yahawah/God: 1 Chronicles 3:17 |* **Priests** = *Called Ministers*

57 and they laid the foundation of the house of God in the first day of the second month, in the second year after *they* were come to Jewry and Jerusalem.

Precept: Jewry = *The country of Judea, Judah: Daniel 5:13 | Luke 23:5 | John 7:1*

58 And they appointed the Levites from twenty years old over the works of the Lord. Then stood *up* Jesus, and his sons and brethren, and Cadmiel *his* brother, and the sons of Madiabun, with the sons of Joda the *son* of Eliadun, with *their* sons and brethren, all Levites, with one accord setters forward of the business, labouring to advance the works in the house of God. So the workmen built the temple of the Lord.

Precept: Cadmiel = *KAD-mih-uhl is the Greek name. His Hebrew name is* **Kadmiel** = *KAD-mih-el; means: God is of old: Ezra 2:40 | Nehemiah 7:43; 12:8 |* **Madiabun** = *much-DIGH-uh-buhn |* **Joda** = *JOH-duh, is the same* **Juda** = *JOO-duh |* **Eliadun** = *ih-LIGH-uh-duhn*

59 And the priests stood arrayed in their vestments with musical *instruments* and trumpets; and the Levites the sons of Asaph had cymbals,

Precept: Asaph = *AY-saf; means: He collected |* **Priests** = *Called Ministers*

60 singing songs of thanksgiving, and praising the Lord, according as David the king of Israel had ordained.

Precept: David = *DAY-vid. The name David is a suggested title to the throne, not a personal name; means: The True Messiah |* **Israel** = *IZ-ray-el; means: A prince of God*

61 And they sung with loud voices songs to the praise of the Lord, because his mercy and glory *is* for ever in all Israel.

Precept: Israel = *IZ-ray-el; means: A prince of God*

62 And all the people sounded trumpets, and shouted with a loud

voice, singing songs of thanksgiving unto the Lord for the rearing up of the house of the Lord.

63 Also of the priests and Levites, and of the chief of their families, the ancients who had seen the former house came to the building of this with weeping and great crying.
Precept: Priests = Called Ministers

64 But many with trumpets and joy *shouted* with loud voice,

65 insomuch that the trumpets might not be heard for the weeping of the people: yet the multitude sounded marvellously, so that *it* was heard afar off.

66 Wherefore when the enemies of the tribe of Judah and Benjamin heard *it*, they came to know what *that* noise of trumpets *should mean*.
Precept: Ezra 4:1-5

67 And they perceived that they that were of the captivity did build the temple unto the Lord God of Israel.
Precept: Israel = IZ-ray-el; means: A prince of God

68 So they went to Zorobabel and Jesus, and to the chief of the families, and said unto them, We will build together with you.
Precept: Zorobabel = zoo-RAHB-uh-buhl, or Zerubbabel = zuh-RUHB-uh-buhl; means: Desendant of Babel

69 For we likewise, as ye, do obey your Lord, and do sacrifice unto him from the days of Azbazareth the king of the Assyrians, who brought us hither.
Precept: Azbazareth = az-BAZ-uh-reth, is Greek. The Hebrew translation is Esarhaddon/Esarhaddon = ee-sahr-HAD-uhn; means: The god Ashur has given a brother | Sacrifice = Prepare; Practice: Genesis 27:17 | Exodus 12:39; 15:2; 23:20 | Numbers 15:5-6; 23:1, 29 | Joshua 1:11 | Psalms 103:9 | Proverbs 8:27 | Jonah 4:6-7 | 1 Esdras 1:13-14 | 2 Esdras 8:60; 9:18 | Practice: Sirach/Ecclesiasticus 10:6 | 2 Peter 2:14

70 Then Zorobabel and Jesus and the chief of the families of Israel said unto them, It is not for us and you to build *together* an house unto the Lord our God.
Precept: **Zorobabel** = *zoo-RAHB-uh-buhl, or* **Zerubbabel** = *zuh-RUHB-uh-buhl; means: Desendant of Babel |* **Israel** = *IZ-ray-el; means: A prince of God*

71 We ourselves alone will build unto the Lord of Israel, according as Cyrus the king of the Persians hath commanded us.
Precept: **Cyrus** = *SIGH-ruhs |* **Persians** = *our-SHANZ: Country laying east of Mesopotamia (modern Iraq) |* **Israel** = *IZ-ray-el; means: A prince of God*

72 But the heathen of the land lying heavy upon the inhabitants of Judea, and holding them strait, hindered their building;
Precept: 1 Chronicles 16:35 | Nehemiah 5:8-9 | Obadiah 1, 2, 15 | **Judea** = *The country of Jewry, County of the Jews: Ezra 5:8 | 1 Esdras 1:26; 2:5, 12 | Tobit 1:18 | Judith 1:12 | 1 Maccabees 4:35 | Matthew 2:5 |* **Strait** = *Narrow, Tight, Difficult, Strict, Rigorous, Constricted: Exodus 13:19 | Isaiah 49:20 | 1 Samuel 13:6 | Judith 4:7; 14:11*

73 and by their secret plots, and popular persuasions and commotions, they hindered the finishing of the building all the time that king Cyrus lived: so they were hindered from building for the space of two years, until the reign of Darius.
Precept: Psalm 64:2 | Ezra 4:5, 6-7, 24 | **Cyrus** = *SIGH-ruhs |* **Darius** = *duh-RIGH-uhs*

1 ESDRAS CHAPTER 6

1 Now in the second year of the reign of Darius Aggeus and Zacharias the son of Addo, the prophets, prophesied unto the Jews in Jewry and Jerusalem in the name of the Lord God of Israel, *which was* upon them.
*Precept: Ezra 5:1 | **Zacharias** = ZAK-uh-RIGH-uhs; means: Yahweh remembers | **Jewry** = The country of Judea, Judah: Daniel 5:13 | Luke 23:5 | John 7:1 | **Darius** = duh-RIGH-uhs | **Aggeus** = AG-ee-uhs, is Greek. His name in Hebrew is **Haggai** = HAG-igh: Haggai 1:1 | **Addo** = AD-oh, is Greek. The translation in Hebrew is **Iddo** = ID-oh: Ezra 5:1 | **Jewry** = The country of Judea, Judah: Daniel 5:13 | Luke 23:5 | John 7:1 | **Israel** = IZ-ray-el; means: A prince of God*

2 Then stood *up* Zorobabel the *son* of Salatiel, and Jesus the *son* of Josedec, and began to build the house of the Lord at Jerusalem, the prophets of the Lord being with them, *and* helping them.
*Precept: **Josedec** = JAHS-uh-dek, or **Jozadak** = JAHZ-uh-dak; means: Yahawah acts in righteousness: 1 Chronicles 6:14-15 | Haggai 1:1 | Ezra 3:2 | **Zorobabel** = zoo-RAHB-uh-buhl, or **Zerubbabel** = zuh-RUHB-uh-buhl; means: Desendant of Babel | **Salatiel** = such-LAY-thih-el; means: I have asked of Yahawah/God: 1 Chronicles 3:17*

3 At the same time came unto them Sisinnes the governor of Syria and Phenice, with Sathrabuzanes and his companions, and said unto them,
*Precept: **Phenice** = fig-NIGH-sih; A town with a harbor on the southern side Crete: Acts 27:12 | **Sisinnes** = sih-SIN-ess, is Greek. The translation is **Tattenai/Tatnai** = TAT-nigh: Ezra 5:3 | **Sathrabuzanes** = saith-rah-BYOO-zuh-neez, is Greek. The translation in Hebrew is **Shethar-boznai** = SHEE-thahr-boz-uh-ni: Ezra 5:3, 6; 6:6*

4 By whose appointment do ye build this house and this roof, and perform all the other *things?* and who are the workmen that perform these *things?*

5 Nevertheless the elders of the Jews obtained favour, because the Lord had visited the captivity;
*Precept: **Elders** = Also Ancients: 1 Esdras 6:5, 11, 27; 7:1 |*

6 And they were not hindered from building, until such time as

signification was given unto Darius concerning them, and an answer received.
Precept: Darius = duh-RIGH-uhs

7 The copy of the letters which Sisinnes, governor of Syria and Phenice, and Sathrabuzanes, with their companions, rulers in Syria and Phenice, wrote and sent unto Darius;
Precept: Phenice = fig-NIGH-sih; A town with a harbor on the southern side Crete: Acts 27:12 | Sisinnes = sih-SIN-ess, is Greek. The translation is Tattenai/Tatnai = TAT-nigh: Ezra 5:3 | Sathrabuzanes = saith-rah-BYOO-zuh-neez, is Greek. The translation in Hebrew is Shethar-boznai = SHEE-thahr-boz-uh-ni: Ezra 5:3, 6; 6:6

8 To king Darius, greeting. Let all *things* be known unto our lord the king, that being come into the country of Judea, and entered into the city of Jerusalem we found in the city of Jerusalem the ancients of the Jews *that were* of the captivity
Precept: Luke 1:39, 65 | Mark 1:5 | Judea = The country of Jewry, County of the Jews: Ezra 5:8 | 1 Esdras 1:26; 2:5, 12 | Tobit 1:18 | Judith 1:12 | 1 Maccabees 4:35 | Matthew 2:5 | Ancients of the Jews = Elder(s): Exodus 3:16 | Ezra 5:5; 6:14 | Luke 7:3 | Genesis 50:7 | Numbers 11:16-17; 22:7 | 1 Samuel 24:13 | Matthew 5:21 | Darius = duh-RIGH-uhs |

9 Building an house unto the Lord, great *and* new, of hewn and costly stones, and the timber *already* laid upon the walls.
Precept: Costly = Expensive | Costly Stones = Sardius, Topaz, Carbuncle, Emerald, Sapphire, Diamond, Ligure, Agate, Amethyst, Beryl, Onyx, and Jasper | 1 Kings 7:10-11; 5:17 | Proverbs 20:15

10 And those works *are* done with great speed, and the work goeth on prosperously in their hands, and with all glory and diligence *is it* made.
Precept: Prosperously = Successfully | Diligence = Of high value, upmost importance: Deuteronomy 4:9; 6:17 | Psalms 77:6; 119:4 | 2 Esdras 9:1; 13:54 | Wisdom 7:13; 13:7 | Sirach/Ecclesiasticus 18:14; 27:3 | Susanna 12 | Proverbs 10:4

11 Then asked we these elders, saying, By whose commandment build ye this house, and lay the foundations of these works?

12 Therefore to the intent that *we* might give knowledge unto thee by writing, we demanded of them who were the chief doers,

and we required of them the names in writing of their principal *men.*
Precept: Principal = Chief(s)

13 So they gave us this answer, We are the servants of the Lord which made heaven and earth.
Precept: Heaven = Firmament Separated from he earth. The color blue of the sky was attributed to the chaotic waters that the firmament is separated: Genesis 1:7 | Deuteronomy 5:8 | Job 26:11 | 2 Samuel 22:8

14 And *as for* this house, *it* was builded many years ago by a king of Israel great and strong, and was finished.
Precept: Israel = IZ-ray-el; means: A prince of God

15 But when our fathers provoked *God* unto wrath, and sinned against the Lord of Israel which is in heaven, he gave them over into the power of Nabuchodonosor king of Babylon, of the Chaldees;
Precept: Babylon = Confuse, Confound; An enormously important city in antiquity ("gate of the god") | Chaldees = Chaldeans | Nabuchodonosor = nab-uh-kuh-DAHN-ub-sawr | Israel = IZ-ray-el; means: A prince of God | Heaven = Firmament Separated from he earth. The color blue of the sky was attributed to the chaotic waters that the firmament is separated: Genesis 1:7 | Deuteronomy 5:8 | Job 26:11 | 2 Samuel 22:8

16 who pulled down the house, and burned *it*, and carried away the people captives unto Babylon.
Precept: Babylon = Confuse, Confound; An enormously important city in antiquity ("gate of the god")

17 But in the first year that king Cyrus reigned over the country of Babylon Cyrus the king wrote to build *up* this house.
Precept: Babylon = Confuse, Confound; An enormously important city in antiquity ("gate of the god") | Precept: Cyrus = SIGH-ruhs

18 And the holy vessels of gold and of silver, that Nabuchodonosor had carried away out of the house at Jerusalem, and had set them in his own temple those Cyrus the king brought forth again out of the temple at Babylon, and they were delivered to Zorobabel and to Sanabassarus the ruler,

48

Precept: Babylon = *Confuse, Confound; An enormously important city in antiquity* *("gate of the god") | Precept: Cyrus* = *SIGH-ruhs | Sanabassarus* = *san-uh-BASS-uh-* *ruhs | Zorobabel* = *zoo-RAHB-uh-buhl, or Zerubbabel* = *zuh-RUHB-uh-buhl; means:* *Desendant of Babel | Nabuchodonosor* = *nab-uh-kuh-DAHN-ub-sawr*

19 with commandment that he should carry away the same vessels, and put them in the temple at Jerusalem; and that the temple of the Lord should be built in his place.

20 Then the same Sanabassarus, being come hither, laid the foundations of the house of the Lord at Jerusalem; and from that *time* to this being still a building, it is not yet fully ended.

21 Now therefore, if it seem good unto the king, let search be made among the records of king Cyrus:
Precept: Cyrus = *SIGH-ruhs | Sanabassarus* = *san-uh-BASS-uh-ruhs | Records* = *The* *Rolls*

22 and if it be found that the building of the house of the Lord at Jerusalem hath been done with the consent of king Cyrus, and if our lord the king be so minded, let him signify unto us thereof.
Precept: Cyrus = *SIGH-ruhs*

23 Then commanded king Darius to seek among the records at Babylon: and *so* at Ecbatane the palace, which is in the country of Media, there was found a roll wherein these *things* were recorded.
Precept: Babylon = *Confuse, Confound; An enormously important city in antiquity* *("gate of the god") | Darius* = *duh-RIGH-uhs | Ecbatane* = *ARK-mathta, is Greek.* *The actual name is in Hebrew Achmetha* = *AK-mee-thuh: Ezra 6:2. Achmetha is* *located in the Zagros mountains of Nw Iran between Tehran and Baghdad.*

24 In the first year of the reign of Cyrus king Cyrus commanded that the house of the Lord at Jerusalem should be built *again,* where they do sacrifice with continual fire:
Precept: Cyrus = *SIGH-ruhs | Sacrifice* = *Prepare; Practice: Genesis 27:17 | Exodus* *12:39; 15:2; 23:20 | Numbers 15:5-6; 23:1, 29 | Joshua 1:11 | Psalms 103:9 |* *Proverbs 8:27 | Jonah 4:6-7 | 1 Esdras 1:13-14 | 2 Esdras 8:60; 9:18 | Practice:* *Sirach/Ecclesiasticus 10:6 | 2 Peter 2:14*

25 Whose height shall be sixty cubits and the breadth sixty cubits, with three rows of hewn stones, and one row of new wood of that country; and the expences *thereof* to be given out of the house of king Cyrus:

Precept: Cyrus = SIGH-ruhs

26 and that the holy vessels of the house of the Lord, both of gold and silver, that Nabuchodonosor took out of the house at Jerusalem, and brought to Babylon, should be restored to the house at Jerusalem, and be set in the place where they were *before*.

Precept: Babylon = Confuse, Confound; An enormously important city in antiquity ("gate of the god") | Nabuchodonosor = nab-uh-kuh-DAHN-ub-sawr

27 And *also* he commanded that Sisinnes the governor of Syria and Phenice, and Sathrabuzanes, and their companions, and those which were appointed rulers in Syria and Phenice, should be careful not to meddle with the place, but suffer Zorobabel, the servant of the Lord, and governor of Judea, and the elders of the Jews, to build the house of the Lord in that place.

Precept: Judea = The country of Jewry, County of the Jews: Ezra 5:8 | 1 Esdras 1:26; 2:5, 12 | Tobit 1:18 | Judith 1:12 | 1 Maccabees 4:35 | Matthew 2:5 | Precept: Phenice = fig-NIGH-sih; A town with a harbor on the southern side Crete: Acts 27:12 | Sisinnes = sih-SIN-ess, is Greek. The translation is Tattenai/Tatnai = TAT-nigh: Ezra 5:3 | Sathrabuzanes = saith-rah-BYOO-zuh-neez, is Greek. The translation in Hebrew is Shethar-boznai = SHEE-thahr-boz-uh-ni: Ezra 5:3, 6; 6:6 | Zorobabel = zoh-RAHB-uh-buhl or Zerubbabel = zuh-RUHB-uh-buhl; means: Seed of Babylon: Ezra 3:2; Haggai 1:1 | Elders = Ancients of the Jews: 1 Esdras 6:5, 11, 27; 7:1 | Exodus 3:16 | Genesis 50:7 | Numbers 11:16-17; 22:7 | 1 Samuel 24:13 | Matthew 5:21

28 I have commanded also to have it built up whole *again*; and that *they* look diligently to help those that be of the captivity of the Jews, till the house of the Lord be finished:

29 and out of the tribute of Celosyria and Phenice a portion carefully to be given these men for the sacrifices of the Lord, *that is*, to Zorobabel the governor, for bullocks, and rams, and lambs;

Precept: Celosyria = SEE-loh-SIHR-ih-uh; A location. The eastern harbor of Corinth: Acts 18:18 | Romans 16:1 | Phenice = fig-NIGH-sih; A town with a harbor on the southern side Crete: Acts 27:12 | Zorobabel = zoh-RAHB-uh-buhl or Zerubbabel =

zuh-RUHB-uh-buhl; means: Seed of Babylon: Ezra 3:2; Haggai 1:1 | **Sacrifice** =
Prepare; Practice: Genesis 27:17 | *Exodus 12:39; 15:2; 23:20* | *Numbers 15:5-6;*
23:1, 29 | *Joshua 1:11* | *Psalms 103:9* | *Proverbs 8:27* | *Jonah 4:6-7* | *1 Esdras*
1:13-14 | *2 Esdras 8:60; 9:18* | *Practice: Sirach/Ecclesiasticus 10:6* | *2 Peter 2:14*

30 and also corn, salt, wine, and oil, *and that* continually every
year without *further* question, according as the priests that be in
Jerusalem shall signify to be daily spent:
Precept: Priests = *Called Ministers*

31 that offerings may be made to the most high God for the king
and for his children, and *that* they may pray for their lives.

32 And he commanded that whosoever should transgress, yea, or
make light of any *thing* afore spoken or written, out of his own
house should a tree be taken, and *he* thereon be hanged, and all
his goods seized for the king.

33 The Lord therefore, whose name is there called upon, utterly
destroy every king and nation, that stretcheth out his hand to
hinder or endamage that house of the Lord in Jerusalem.

34 I Darius the king have ordained that according unto these
things it be done with diligence.
Precept: Darius = *duh-RIGH-uhs* | **Diligence** = *Of high value, upmost importance:*
Deuteronomy 4:9; 6:17 | *Psalms 77:6; 119:4* | *2 Esdras 9:1; 13:54* | *Wisdom 7:13;*
13:7 | *Sirach/Ecclesiasticus 18:14; 27:3* | *Susanna 12* | *Proverbs 10:4*

1 ESDRAS CHAPTER 7

1 Then Sisinnes the governor of Celosyria and Phenice, and Sathrabuzanes, with *their* companions following the commandments of king Darius,

Precept: Celosyria = SEE-loh-SIHR-ih-uh; A location. The eastern harbor of Corinth: Acts 18:18 | Romans 16:1 | Phenice = fig-NIGH-sih; A town with a harbor on the southern side Crete: Acts 27:12 | Darius = duh-RIGH-uhs | Sisinnes = sih-SIN-ess, is Greek. The translation is Tattenai/Tatnai = TAT-nigh: Ezra 5:3 | Sathrabuzanes = saith-rah-BYOO-zuh-neez, is Greek. The translation in Hebrew is Shethar-boznai = SHEE-thahr-boz-uh-ni: Ezra 5:3, 6; 6:6

2 did very carefully oversee the holy works, assisting the ancients of the Jews and governors of the temple.

3 And *so* the holy works prospered, when Aggeus and Zacharias the prophets prophesied.

Precept: Zacharias = ZAK-uh-RIGH-uhs; means: Yahweh remembers | Aggeus = AG-ee-uhs, is Greek. His name in Hebrew is Haggai = HAG-igh: Haggai 1:1 | Prophet = A prophet of God is one who has authority and who has the qualifications to convey God's messages to men. Being God's mouth piece. A prophet interpret scripture Parables, Riddles, and dark speeches, giving one the Oracles and the mystery of God word: Jeremiah 3:15; 44:4 | 2 Kings 17:13 | 1 Chronicles 16:22 | Psalms 105:15 | 2 Esdras 1:32 | Matthew 13:35

4 And they finished these *things* by the commandment of the Lord God of Israel, and with the consent of Cyrus, Darius, and Artexerxes, kings of Persia.

Precept: Cyrus = SIGH-ruhs | Artexerxes = ar-TAKS-urk'-sez (Ezra 7:1 | Nehemiah 2:1) | Darius = duh-RIGH-uhs | Persia = PUHR-zhuh: Country laying east of Mesopotamia (modern Iraq) | Israel = IZ-ray-el; means: A prince of God

5 *And thus* was the holy house finished in the three and twentieth day of the month Adar, in the sixth year of Darius king of the Persians.

Precept: Darius = duh-RIGH-uhs | Persians = our-SHANZ: Country laying east of Mesopotamia (Modern Iraq)

6 And the children of Israel, the priests, and the Levites, and others that were of the captivity, that were added *unto them*, did

according to the *things written* in the book of Moses.
Precept: Israel = *IZ-ray-el; means: A prince of God* | **Priests** = *Called Ministers*

7 And to the dedication of the temple of the Lord they offered an hundred bullocks two hundred rams, four hundred lambs;

8 and twelve goats for the sin of all Israel, according to the number of the chief of the tribes of Israel.
Precept: Israel = *IZ-ray-el; means: A prince of God*

9 The priests also and the Levites stood arrayed in their vestments, according to their kindreds, in the service of the Lord God of Israel, according to the book of Moses: and the porters at every gate.
Precept: Israel = *IZ-ray-el; means: A prince of God* | **Priests** = *Called Ministers* | **Vestments** = *Priestly or Garments, Apparel, Raiment, and Clothing:2 Kings 10:22* | *Exodus 39:1* | *Sirach/Ecclesiasticus 45:10* | *2 Maccabees 3:15*

10 And the children of Israel that were of the captivity held the passover the fourteenth *day* of the first month, after that the priests and the Levites were sanctified.
Precept: Passover: Exodus 12:5-6 | *Leviticus 23:5* | *Numbers 9:5; 28:16* | *Joshua 5:10* | *Ezra 6:19* | **Israel** = *IZ-ray-el; means: A prince of God* | **Priests** = *Called Ministers*

11 They that were of the captivity were not all sanctified together: but the Levites were all sanctified together.

12 And *so* they offered the passover for all them of the captivity, and for their brethren the priests, and for themselves.
Precept: Passover: Exodus 12:5-6 | *Leviticus 23:5* | *Numbers 9:5; 28:16* | *Joshua 5:10* | *Ezra 6:19* | **Priests** = *Called Ministers* | **Brethren** = *breth-ran: means: Referring to the members of a Sect, society, or of Profession. Many times used as Brother: Genesis 9:22, 25; 19:7* | *Deuteronomy 3:20; 10:9* | *1 Esdras 8:47* | *Tobit 1:3*

13 And the children of Israel that *came* out of the captivity did eat, *even* all they that had separated themselves from the abominations of the people of the land, and sought the Lord.
Precept: Abominations = *Repugnant, detestable act, person or thing. Corrupted, Polluted, Abhorrent, loathsome, unclean, and rejected; Most hated: Exodus 8:26* |

*Deuteronomy 7:25; 17:1; 18:12 | Proverbs 6:16; 20:23; 28:9 | Psalms 119:163 | Sirach/Ecclesiasticus 13:20; 20:8 | Amos 5:10; 6:8 | **Israel** = IZ-ray-el; means: A prince of God*

14 And they kept the feast of unleavened bread seven days, making merry before the Lord,

15 For that he had turned the counsel of the king of Assyria toward them, to strengthen their hands in the works of the Lord God of Israel.

*⋀Precept: **Assyria** = uh-SIHR-ih-uh. Ancient empire seen as the symbol of terror and tyranny. Assyria received its name from the tiny city-state Asshur, on the western bank of the Tigris River in the northern Mesopotamia (modern Iraq). The Hebrew name occurs frequently in the scriptures and translated Assyria you will see (Genesis 2;14), Assur (Ezra 4:2 and Psalm 83:8) | **Israel** = IZ-ray-el; means: A prince of God*

1 ESDRAS CHAPTER 8

1 And after these *things*, when Artexerxes the king of the Persians reigned came Esdras *the son* of Saraias, the *son* of Ezerias, the *son* of Helchiah, the *son* of Salum,

Precept: Artexerxes = ar-TAKS-urk'-sez | Saraias = such-RAY-yuhs; means: Yahawah has persevered or persisted | Salum = SAY-luhm, and Shallum = SHAL-uhm; means: Replacer: Ezra Ezra 7:2 | Persians = our-SHANZ: Country laying east of Mesopotamia (modern Iraq) | Esdras = Ez-druhs, is Greek. The Hebrew translation is Ezra = Ez-ruh; means: Yahawah is my help | Ezerias = ez-uh-RIGH-uhs, is Greek. The Hebrew translation is Azariah = az-uh-RIGH-uh; means: Yahawah has helped: 1 Kings 4:2 | Helchiah = hehl-KIGH-uh, is Greek. The Hebrew translation is Hilkiah = his-KIGH-uh; means: My portion is Yahawah: 1 Chronicles 6:30

2 the *son* of Sadduc, the *son* of Achitob, the *son* of Amarias, the *son* of Ozias, the *son* of Memeroth, the *son* of Zaraias, the *son* of Savias, the *son* of Boccas, the *son* of Abisum, the *son* of Phinees, the *son* of Eleazar, the *son* of Aaron the chief priest.

Precept: Phinees = Fin-ih-uhs is Greek. His Hebrew name is Phinehas = FIN-ih-huhs; means: Dark-skinned one. One of Ezra's progenitors: 2 Esdras 1:2. However, this link is not found in Ezra's genealogy checking 1 Esdras 8:1, Ezra 7:1, or 1 Chronicles chapter 6. this will be found in 2 Esdras 1:2, Ezra's descent was from Eleazar, while Phinees (Phinehas) was a direct descendant of Ithamar, the youngest son of Aaron | Sadduc = SAD-uhk, is Greek. The Hebrew translation is Zadok = ZAY-dahk: 2 Samuel 8:17 | Achitob = AK-uh-tahb, is Greek. The Hebrew translation is Ahitub = uh-HIGH-tuhb: 1 Samuel 14:3; 22:9 | Amarias = am-uh-RIGH-uhs, is Greek. The Hebrew translation is Amariah = am-uh-RIGH-uh; means: The Lord has spoken, The lord has promised: 1 Chronicles 5:33-34; 6:37-37 | Ozias = oh-ZIGH-uhs, is Greek. The Hebrew translation is Uzziah = uh-ZIGH-uh; means: Yahawah is my strength: 2 Chronicles 26:8. This name has a alternative form is Azariah = az-uh-RIGH-uh | Memeroth = mem-ER-oth. This name have another spelling; Meraioth = mid-RAY-ahth; means: Rebellions: Ezra 7:3 | Zaraias = zh-Ray-yuhs, is Greek. The Hebrew translation is Seraiah = sih-RIGH-uh; means: Yahawah has prevailed: 2 Samuel 8:17 | Ezra 2:2 | Savias = such-VIGH-uhs, is Greek. The Hebrew translation is Uzzi = UHZ-igh; means: The might of Yahawah; Power of the Lord | Boccas = BAHK-uhs, is Greek. The translation in Hebrew has two versions; 1. Bukkiah = buh-KIGH-uh in 1 Chronicles 25:4 and a shorten version of the name "Bukki = BUHK-igh: 1 Chronicles 5:31; Ezra 7:4 | Abisum = uh-BIGH-suhm, is Greek. The Hebrew translation is Abishua = uh-BIGH-suhm; means: My father is deliverance: Ezra 7:5 | Aaron = EHR-uhn; means: Mountaineer, Enlightened

3 This Esdras went up from Babylon, as a scribe, being very ready in the law of Moses, that was given by the God of Israel.

*Precept: Esdras = Ez-druhs, is Greek. The Hebrew translation is **Ezra** = Ez-ruh; means: Yahawah is my help*

4 And the king did him honour: for he found grace in his sight in all his requests.

5 There went up with him also *certain* of the children of Israel, of the priest of the Levites, of the holy singers, porters, and ministers of the temple, unto Jerusalem,
*Precept: **Ministers** = Called Priests: Joel 1:9, 13 | Numbers 3:3 | Ezra 8:17 | Psalm 103:21*

6 in the seventh year of the reign of Artexerxes, in the fifth month, this was the king's seventh year; for they went from Babylon in the first day of the first month, and came to Jerusalem, according to the prosperous journey which the Lord gave them.
*Precept: **Artexerxes** = ar-TAKS-urk'-sez | **Babylon** = Confuse, Confound; An enormously important city in antiquity ("gate of the god")*

7 For Esdras had very great skill, so that *he* omitted nothing of the law and commandments of the Lord, but taught all Israel the ordinances and judgments.
*Precept: **Esdras** = Ez-druhs, is Greek. The Hebrew translation is **Ezra** = Ez-ruh; means: Yahawah is my help | **Ordinances** = Order, specific directions, seen as Law of direction: Exodus 18:20 | Leviticus 18:3, 30*

8 Now the copy of the commission, which was written from Artexerxes the king, and came to Esdras the priest and reader of the law of the Lord, is this that followeth;
*Precept: **Artexerxes** = ar-TAKS-urk'-sez | **Esdras** = Ez-druhs, is Greek. The Hebrew translation is **Ezra** = Ez-ruh; means: Yahawah is my help*

9 King Artexerxes unto Esdras the priest and reader of the law of the Lord *sendeth* greeting:
*Precept: **Artexerxes** = ar-TAKS-urk'-sez | **Esdras** = Ez-druhs, is Greek. The Hebrew translation is **Ezra** = Ez-ruh; means: Yahawah is my help*

10 having determined to deal graciously, I have given order, that

such of the nation of the Jews, and of the priests and Levites being within our realm, as are willing and desirous should go with thee unto Jerusalem.

Precept: Priests = *Called Ministers*

11 As many therefore as have a mind *thereunto*, let them depart with thee, as it hath seemed good both to me and my seven friends the counsellors;

12 that they may look unto the *affairs* of Judea and Jerusalem, agreeably to *that* which is in the law of the Lord;

Precept: Judea = *The country of Jewry, County of the Jews: Ezra 5:8 | 1 Esdras 1:26; 2:5, 12 | Tobit 1:18 | Judith 1:12 | 1 Maccabees 4:35 | Matthew 2:5*

13 and carry the gifts unto the Lord of Israel to Jerusalem, which I and *my* friends have vowed, and all the gold and silver that in the country of Babylon can be found, to the Lord in Jerusalem,

Precept: Babylon = *Confuse, Confound; An enormously important city in antiquity ("gate of the god")*

14 with that *also* which is given of the people for the temple of the Lord their God at Jerusalem: and that silver and gold may be collected for bullocks, rams, and lambs, and *things* thereunto appertaining;

Precept: Appertaineth/Appertain = *ap-er-tan; means: Only once, It becometh, It is seemly, pertain, and It is Thy honor: Jeremiah 10:7 | Leviticus 6:5 | Nehemiah 2:8*

15 to the end that *they* may offer sacrifices unto the Lord upon the altar of the Lord their God, which is in Jerusalem.

Precept: Sacrifice = *Prepare; Practice: Genesis 27:17 | Exodus 12:39; 15:2; 23:20 | Numbers 15:5-6; 23:1, 29 | Joshua 1:11 | Psalms 103:9 | Proverbs 8:27 | Jonah 4:6-7 | 1 Esdras 1:13-14 | 2 Esdras 8:60; 9:18 | Practice: Sirach/Ecclesiasticus 10:6 | 2 Peter 2:14*

16 And whatsoever thou and thy brethren will do with the silver and gold, *that* do, according to the will of thy God.

Precept: Brethren = *breth-ran: means: Referring to the members of a Sect, society, or of Profession. Many times used as Brother: Genesis 9:22, 25; 19:7 | Deuteronomy 3:20; 10:9 | 1 Esdras 8:47 | Tobit 1:3*

17 And the holy vessels of the Lord, which are given thee for the use of the temple of thy God, which is in Jerusalem, thou shalt set before thy God in Jerusalem.

18 And whatsoever *thing* else thou shalt remember for the use of the temple of thy God, thou shalt give *it* out of the king's treasury.

19 And I king Artexerxes have also commanded the keepers of the treasures in Syria and Phenice, that whatsoever Esdras the priest and the reader of the law of the most high God shall send for, they should give *it* him with speed,

Precept: **Phenice** = *fig-NIGH-sih; A town with a harbor on the southern side Crete: Acts 27:12* | **Artexerxes** = *ar-TAKS-urk'-sez* | **Esdras** = *Ez-druhs, is Greek. The Hebrew translation is* **Ezra** = *Ez-ruh; means: Yahawah is my help*

20 to the sum of an hundred talents of silver, likewise also of wheat even to an hundred cors, and an hundred pieces of wine, and other *things* in abundance.

Precept: **Cors/Kors** = *Measure in equivalence to (10 baths, weight, or liquid(s)*

21 Let all *things* be performed after the law of God diligently unto the most high God, that wrath come not upon the kingdom of the king and his sons.

22 I command you also, that ye require no tax, nor any other imposition, of any of the priests, or Levites, or holy singers, or porters, or ministers of the temple, or of any that have doings in this temple, and that no *man* have authority to impose any *thing* upon them.

Precept: **Ministers** = *Called Priests: Joel 1:9, 13* | *Numbers 3:3* | *Ezra 8:17* | *Psalm 103:21* | **Imposition** = *Deception*

23 And thou, Esdras, according to the wisdom of God ordain judges and justices, that they may judge in all Syria and Phenice all those that know the law of thy God; and those that know it not

thou shalt teach.

Precept: **Phenice** = *fig-NIGH-sih; A town with a harbor on the southern side Crete: Acts 27:12* | **Esdras** = *Ez-druhs, is Greek. The Hebrew translation is* **Ezra** = *Ez-ruh; means: Yahawah is my help* | **Ordain** = *Appointed, Establish*

24 And whosoever shall transgress the law of thy God, and of the king, shall be punished diligently, whether *it be* by death, or *other* punishment, by penalty of money, or by imprisonment.

25 Then said Esdras the scribe, Blessed be the only Lord God of my fathers, who hath put these *things* into the heart of the king, to glorify his house that is in Jerusalem:

Precept: **Esdras** = *Ez-druhs, is Greek. The Hebrew translation is* **Ezra** = *Ez-ruh; means: Yahawah is my help* | **Blessed** = *Knowledge of God, All things, Giving knowledge of, Works, The Heavenly Gift of Knowledge, give understanding and knowledge of Blessed = Hallowed, Joined to, Joined, Give, Joined together, Gave knowledge to, Commanded , Praised, Holy, Render, Named Bless = Worship, Give, will Give, Will give you, give us a, praise, Nehemiah 9:5* | *Genesis 1:22* | *Psalm 33:12* | *2 Esdras 13:24*

26 and hath honoured me in the sight of the king, and *his* counsellors, and all his friends and nobles.

27 Therefore was I encouraged by the help of the Lord my God, and gathered together men of Israel to go up with me.

28 And these are the chief according to their families and several dignities, that went up with me from Babylon in the reign of king Artexerxes:

Precept: **Babylon** = *Confuse, Confound; An enormously important city in antiquity ("gate of the god")* | **Artexerxes** = *ar-TAKS-urk'-sez* | **Dignities** = *dig-ni-tiz; means Glorious ones, What honor, Preeminent in power: Genesis 49:3* | *Esther 6:3* | *Ecclesiastes 10:6* | *2 Peter 2:10*

29 of the sons of Phinees, Gerson: of the sons of Ithamar, Gamael: of the sons of David, Lettus the *son* of Sechenias:

Precept: **Phinees** = *Fin-ih-uhs is Greek. His Hebrew name is* **Phinehas** = *FIN-ih-huhs; means: Dark-skinned one. One of Ezra's progenitors: 2 Esdras 1:2. However, this link is not found in Ezra's genealogy checking 1 Esdras 8:1, Ezra 7:1, or 1 Chronicles chapter 6. this will be found in 2 Esdras 1:2, Ezra's descent was from Eleazar, while Phinees (Phinehas) was a direct descendant of Ithamar, the youngest* *son of Aaron* | **Ithamar** = *ITH-uh-mahr; means: Island of palms* | **Gamael** = *GAM-ay-el, the alternate name for Daniel: Ezra 8:2* | **David** = *DAY-vid. The name David is a suggested title to the throne, not a personal name; means: The True Messiah* | **Lettus** = *LET-uhs* | **Sechenias** = *sek-uh-NIGH-uhs, is Greek. The Hebrew translation is* **Shecaniah** = *shek-uh-NIGH-uh: 1 Chronicles 24:11*

30 of the sons of Pharez, Zacharias; and with him were counted an hundred and fifty men:

Precept: **Zacharias** = *ZAK-uh-RIGH-uhs; means: Yahweh remembers* | **Zacharias** = *ZAK-uh-RIGH-uhs; means: Yahweh remembers*

31 of the sons of Pahath Moab, Eliaonias, *the son* of Zaraias, and with him two hundred men:

Precept: **Phaath Moab** = *PAY-hath-MOH-ab; means: Governor of Moab, also found under the name Eliehoenai: Ezra 8:4* | *1 Esdras 8:31* | **Eliaonias** = *ih-ligh-oh-NIgH-uhs, is Greek. The Hebrew translation is* **Elioenai** = *el-ih-oh-EE-nigh; means: My eyes (are turned) toward Yahawah: 1 Chronicles 3:23-24* | **Zaraias** = *huh-RAY-yuhs, is Greek. The Hebrew translation is* **Seraiah** = *sih-RIGH-uh; means: The LORD persists: 1 Chronicles 4:13*

32 of the sons of Zathoe, Sechenias *the son* of Jezelus, and with him three hundred men: of the sons of Adin, Obeth *the son* of Jonathan, and with him two hundred and fifty men:

Precept: **Sechenias** = *sek-uh-NIGH-uhs, is Greek. The Hebrew translation is* **Shecaniah** = *shek-uh-NIGH-uh: 1 Chronicles 24:11* | **Zathoe** = *ZATH-oh-ee, is Greek. The Hebrew translation is* **Zattu** = *ZAT-oo: Ezra 2:8* | *Nehemiah 7:13* | **Jezelus** = *JEZ-uh-luhs. In Ezra 8:5,* **Jezelus** *is* **Jahaziel** = *huh-HAY-zih-el; in Ezra 8:9,* **Jehiel**, *means: El sees* | **Adin** = *AY-din; means Luxury, Delight* | **Obeth** = *OH-beth. The Hebrew translation is* **Obed** = *OH-bed; means: Worshiper, Servant; Serving servant: Ruth 4:13* | **Jonathan** = *JAHN-uh-thuhn; means: Yahawah has given*

33 of the sons of Elam, Josias *son* of Gotholias, and with him seventy men:

Precept: **Josias** = *Joh-SIGH-uhs is the Greek translation. The Hebrew name is* **Josiah** = *Joh-SIGH-uh; means: The root of this comes from Yahawah brings forth, to heal: 2 Kings 21:23-24* | **Elam** = *EE-luhm; means Highland* | **Gotholias** = *Garth-uh-LIGH-uhs, is Greek. The Hebrew translation is* **Athaliah** = *auth-uh-LIGH-uh; means Yahawah is exalted. A woman: 2 Kings 11:1*

34 of the sons of Saphatias, Zaraias *son* of Michael, and with him threescore and ten men:

Precept: **Saphatias** = *san-uh-TIGH-uhs. The Hebrew translation is* **Shephatiah** = *chef-uh-TIGH-uh; means: The LORD has judge: 1 Chronicles 27:16* | *1 Chronicles 3:3*

| **Zaraias** = huh-RAY-yuhs. *The Hebrew translation is* **Seraiah** = sih-RIGH-uh: *1 Chronicles 4:13-14* | *Ezra 2:2; 7:1* | **Michael** = MIGH-kuhl; *means: Who is like God*

35 of the sons of Joab, Abadias *son* of Jezelus, and with him two hundred and twelve men:

Precept: Joab = JOH-ab; *means: Yahawah is Father* | **Abadias** = ab-uh-DIGH-uhs. *The Hebrew translation is* **Obadiah** = oh-buh-DIGH-uh; *means: servant of Yahawah* | **Jezelus** = JEZ-uh-luhs. *In Ezra 8:5,* **Jezelus** *is* **Jahaziel** = huh-HAY-zih-el; **Jezelus** *is Jehiel in Ezra 8:9; means: El sees*

36 of the sons of Banid, Assalimoth *son* of Josaphias, and with him an hundred and threescore men:

Precept: Banid = BAN-id, *is a Greek name. The translation is* **Bani** = BAY-nigh; *means: Yahawah has built: 2 Samuel 23:36* | **Assalimoth** = uh-SAL-uh-mahth. *The Hebrew translation is* **Shelomith** = shih-LOH-mith, *used by both men and women: Leviticus 24:11* | *Ezra 8:10* | **Josaphias** = Joh-sah-FIGH-uhs. *The Hebrew translation is* **Josiphiah** = jays-ih-FIGH-uh; *means: Yah adds to: Ezra 8:10*

37 of the sons of Babi, Zacharias *son* of Bebai, and with him twenty and eight men:

Precept: Zacharias = ZAK-uh-RIGH-uhs; *means: Yahwah remembers* | **Babi** = BAY-bigh. *The Hebrew translation is* **Bebai** = BEE-bigh; *means: Child: Ezra 2:11; 8:11* |

38 of the sons of Astath, Johannes *son of* Acatan, and with him an hundred and ten men:

Precept: Astath = ASS-tath. *The Hebrew translation is* **Azgad** = AZ-gad; *means: Gad is mighty, or Gad is strong: Ezra 2:12* | *Nehemiah 7:17* | **Johannes** = John-HAN-iz | **Acatan** = AK-uh-tan. *The Hebrew translation is* **Hakkatan** = HAK-uh-tan; *means: The small one: Ezra 8:12*

39 of the sons of Adonikam the last, and these are the names of them, Eliphalet, Jeuel, and Samaias, and with them seventy men:

Precept: Adonikam = ad-oh-NIGH-kuhm; *means: the Lord has arisen: Ezra 2:13; 8:13* | **Eliphalet** = ih-LIF-uh-let. *The Hebrew translation is* **Eliphelet** = ih-LIF-eh-let; *means: El [God] is deliverance, The divine deliverer: 1 Chronicles 3:6* | **Jeuel** = JOO-el. *The Hebrew translation is* **Jeiel** = jih-IGH; *means El [God] takes away: 1 Chronicles 5:7* | **Samaias** = such-MAY-yuhs. *The Hebrew translation is* **Shemaiah** = shih-MAY-yuh; *means: The LORD has heard: 1 Kings 12:22*

40 of the sons of Bago, Uthi the *son* of Istalcurus, and with him seventy men.

Precept: Bago = BAY-goh. *The Hebrew translation is* **Bigvai** = BIG-vay-igh; *means:*

*Happy: Ezra 2:2 | Nehemiah 7:7 | **Uthi** = oo-THI. The Hebrew translation is **Uthai** = YOO-thigh; means: Pride of the LORD: Ezra 8:14 | **Istalcurus** = iss-tuhl-KYOOR-uhs*

41 And these I gathered together to the river called Theras, where we pitched our tents three days: and *then* I surveyed them.

Precept: Theras = THEE-ruhs. *The river by which the company assembled in preparation for the march to river actual named Ahava: Ezra 8:21, 31*

42 But when I had found there none of the priests and Levites,

Precept: Priests = Called Ministers

43 then sent I unto Eleazar, and Iduel, and Masman,

Precept: Eleazar = E-ih-AY-zuhr; means: God has helped | **Iduel** = IHD-yoo-el. *The Hebrew translation is **Ariel** = EHR-ih-el; having a wide range of meanings: lion[ness] of God: Isaiah 29:1-2, 7. Ezra 8:16 means; Altar heart, Heroes | **Masman** = MASS-man; means: Man of understanding*

44 and Alnathan, and Mamaias, and Joribus, *and* Nathan, Eunatan, Zacharias, and Mosollamus, principal *men* and learned.

Precept: Zacharias = ZAK-uh-RIGH-uhs; means: Yahweh remembers | **Alnathan** = al-NAY-thuhn. *The Hebrew translation is **Elanthan** = el-NAY-thuhn; means: God has given: Jeremiah 36:12 | **Mamaias** = much-MAY-yuhs. The Hebrew translation is **Shemaiah** = shih-MAY-yuh; means: The LORD heard: 2 Chronicles 11:2 | **Joribus** = juh-RIGH-buhs. He is called **Jarib** = JAY-rib in Ezra 8:16; means: Strive, contend | **Nathan** = NAY-thuhn; means Gift | **Eunatan** = yoo-NAY-tuhn | **Zacharias** = ZAK-uh-RIGH-uhs; means: Yahweh remembers | **Mosollamus** = MO-sol-LAM-us. The Hebrew translation is **Meshullam** = mi-shool-uhm; means: Reconciled, perfect: 1 Chronicles 8:17*

45 And I bade them that *they* should go unto Saddeus the captain, who was in the place of the treasury:

Precept: Saddeus = SAD-ih-uhs. *The etymological name is **Iddo**, or **Yiddo**.*

46 and commanded them that *they* should speak unto Daddeus, and to his brethren, and to the treasurers in *that* place, to send us such *men* as might execute the priests' office in the house of the Lord.

Precept: Daddeus = DAD-ih-uhs | **Priests** = Called Ministers | **Brethren** = breth-ran: *means: Referring to the members of a Sect, society, or of Profession. Many times used as Brother: Genesis 9:22, 25; 19:7 | Deuteronomy 3:20; 10:9 | 1 Esdras 8:47 | Tobit 1:3*

47 And by the mighty hand of our Lord they brought unto us skilful men of the sons of Moli the *son* of Levi, the *son* of Israel, Asebebia, and his sons, and *his* brethren, who were eighteen.

Precept: Moli = MOH-ligh. The Hebrew translation is Mahli = MA-ligh; means: be weak, sick | Levi = LEE-vigh; means: a joining | Israel = IZ-ray-el; means: A prince of God | Asebebia = ass-uh-BEE-bee-uh; means: The Lord has sent severe heat | Brethren = breth-ran: means: Referring to the members of a Sect, society, or of Profession. Many times used as Brother: Genesis 9:22, 25; 19:7 | Deuteronomy 3:20; 10:9 | 1 Esdras 8:47 | Tobit 1:3

48 And Asebia, and Annuus, and Osaias *his* brother, of the sons of Channuneus, and their sons, *were* twenty men.

Precept: Asebia = uh-SEE-bee-uh | Annuus = AN-yoo-uhs | Osaias = oh-SAY-yuhs. The Hebrew translation is Jeshaiah or Isaiah = igh (eye) | Channuneus = Kan-uh-NEE-uhs

49 And of the servants of the temple whom David had ordained, and the principal *men* for the service of the Levites *to wit*, the servants of the temple two hundred and twenty, the catalogue of whose names were shewed.

Precept: David = DAY-vid. The name David is a suggested title to the throne, not a personal name; means: The True Messiah

50 And there I vowed a fast unto the young men before our Lord, to desire of him a prosperous journey both for us and them that were with us, for our children, and for the cattle:

51 for I was ashamed to ask the king footmen, and horsemen, and conduct for safeguard against our adversaries.

52 For we had said unto the king, that the power of the Lord our God should be with them that seek him, to support them in all ways.

53 And again we besought our Lord as touching these *things*, and found him favourable *unto us*.

54 Then I separated twelve of the chief of the priests, Esebrias,

and Assanias, and ten men of their brethren with them:

Precept: **Esebrias** = *es-ih-BRIGH-uhs* | **Assanias** = *ass-uh-NIGH-uhs* | **Priests** = *Called Ministers* | **Brethren** = *breth-ran: means: Referring to the members of a Sect, society, or of Profession. Many times used as Brother: Genesis 9:22, 25; 19:7 | Deuteronomy 3:20; 10:9 | 1 Esdras 8:47 | Tobit 1:3*

55 and I weighed them the gold, and the silver, and the holy vessels of the house of our Lord, which the king, and his council, and the princes, and all Israel, had given.

56 And when I had weighed *it*, I delivered unto them six hundred and fifty talents of silver, and silver vessels of an hundred talents, and an hundred talents of gold,

57 and twenty golden vessels, and twelve vessels of brass, *even* of fine brass, glittering like gold.

58 And I said unto them, Both ye are holy unto the Lord, and the vessels are holy, and the gold and the silver *is* a vow unto the Lord, the Lord of our fathers.

59 Watch ye, and keep *them* till ye deliver them to the chief of the priests and Levites, and to the principal *men* of the families of Israel, in Jerusalem, into the chambers of the house of our God.

Precept: **Israel** = *IZ-ray-el; means: A prince of God* | **Priests** = *Called Ministers*

60 So the priests and the Levites, who had received the silver and the gold and the vessels, brought *them* unto Jerusalem, into the temple of the Lord.

Precept: **Priests** = *Called Ministers*

61 And from the river Theras we departed the twelfth day of the first month, and came to Jerusalem by the mighty hand of our Lord, which was with us: and from the beginning of our journey the Lord delivered us from every enemy, and *so* we came to Jerusalem.

Precept: **Theras** = *THEE-ruhs. The river by which the company assembled in preparation for the march to river actual named Ahava: Ezra 8:21, 31*

62 And when we had been there three days, the gold and silver *that wa*s weighed was delivered in the house of our Lord on the fourth day unto Marmoth the priest *the son* of Iri.
Precept: Marmoth = MAHR-mahht; means; Heights | Iri = iGH(eye); means: My city, My town

63 And with him was Eleazar the *son* of Phinees, and with them were Josabad *the son* of Jesu and Moeth *the son* of Sabban, Levites: all *was delivered them* by number and weight.
Precept: Phinees = Fin-ih-uhs is Greek. His Hebrew name is Phinehas = FIN-ih-huhs; means: Dark-skinned one. One of Ezra's progenitors: 2 Esdras 1:2. However, this link is not found in Ezra's genealogy checking 1 Esdras 8:1, Ezra 7:1, or 1 Chronicles chapter 6. this will be found in 2 Esdras 1:2, Ezra's descent was from Eleazar, while Phinees (Phinehas) was a direct descendant of Ithamar, the youngest son of Aaron | Eleazar = E-ih-AY-zuhr; means: God has helped | Josabad = JAHS=uh-bad; means: the LORD is a gift, or The LORD has given | Jesu = JEH-soo | Moeth = MOH-eth. An alternate form of the name of Noadiah = not-uh-DIGH-uh: means; Appear: Ezra 8:33 | Sabban = SAB-an

64 And all the weight of them was written *up* the same hour.

65 Moreover they that were come out of the captivity offered sacrifice unto the Lord God of Israel, *even* twelve bullocks for all Israel, fourscore and sixteen rams,
Precept: Sacrifice = Prepare; Practice: Genesis 27:17 | Exodus 12:39; 15:2; 23:20 | Numbers 15:5-6; 23:1, 29 | Joshua 1:11 | Psalms 103:9 | Proverbs 8:27 | Jonah 4:6-7 | 1 Esdras 1:13-14 | 2 Esdras 8:60; 9:18 | Practice: Sirach/Ecclesiasticus 10:6 | 2 Peter 2:14

66 threescore and twelve lambs, goats for a peace offering, twelve; all of them a sacrifice to the Lord.
Precept: Sacrifice = Prepare; Practice: Genesis 27:17 | Exodus 12:39; 15:2; 23:20 | Numbers 15:5-6; 23:1, 29 | Joshua 1:11 | Psalms 103:9 | Proverbs 8:27 | Jonah 4:6-7 | 1 Esdras 1:13-14 | 2 Esdras 8:60; 9:18 | Practice: Sirach/Ecclesiasticus 10:6 | 2 Peter 2:14

67 And they delivered the king's commandments unto the king's stewards' and to the governors of Celosyria and Phenice; and they honoured the people and the temple of God.
Precept: Celosyria = SEE-loh-SIHR-ih-uh; A location. The eastern harbor of Corinth:

*Acts 18:18 | Romans 16:1 | **Phenice** = fig-NIGH-sih; A town with a harbor on the southern side Crete: Acts 27:12*

68 Now when these *things* were done, the rulers came unto me, and said,

69 The nation of Israel, the princes, the priests and Levites, have not put away *from them* the strange people of the land, nor the pollutions of the Gentiles *to wit*, of the Canaanites, Hittites, Pheresites, Jebusites, and the Moabites, Egyptians, and Edomites.
***Precept: Israel** = IZ-ray-el; means: A prince of God | **Canaanites** = KAY-nuhn-ight | **Priests** = Called Ministers*

70 For both they and their sons have married with their daughters, and the holy seed is mixed with the strange people of the land; and from the beginning of *this* matter the rulers and the great men have been partakers of this iniquity.

71 And as soon as I had heard these *things*, I rent *my* clothes, and the holy garment, and pulled off the hair from off *my* head and beard, and sat me down sad and very heavy.

72 So *all* they that were then moved at the word of the Lord God of Israel assembled unto me, whilst I mourned for the iniquity: but I sat still full of heaviness until the evening sacrifice.
***Precept: Sacrifice** = Prepare; Practice: Genesis 27:17 | Exodus 12:39; 15:2; 23:20 | Numbers 15:5-6; 23:1, 29 | Joshua 1:11 | Psalms 103:9 | Proverbs 8:27 | Jonah 4:6-7 | 1 Esdras 1:13-14 | 2 Esdras 8:60; 9:18 | Practice: Sirach/Ecclesiasticus 10:6 | 2 Peter 2:14*

73 Then rising up from the fast with *my* clothes and the holy garment rent, and bowing *my* knees, and stretching forth *my* hands unto the Lord,

74 I said, O Lord, I am confounded and ashamed before thy face;

75 For our sins are multiplied above our heads, and our ignorances have reached up unto heaven.

Precept: Heaven = *Firmament Separated from he earth. The color blue of the sky was attributed to the chaotic waters that the firmament is separated: Genesis 1:7 | Deuteronomy 5:8 | Job 26:11 | 2 Samuel 22:8*

76 for ever since the time of our fathers we *have been* and are in great sin, *even* unto this day.

77 And for our sins and our fathers' we with our brethren and our kings and our priests were given up unto the kings of the earth, to the sword, and *to* captivity, and *for* a prey with shame, unto this day.

Precept: Priests = *Called Ministers* | *Brethren* = *breth-ran: means: Referring to the members of a Sect, society, or of Profession. Many times used as Brother: Genesis 9:22, 25; 19:7 | Deuteronomy 3:20; 10:9 | 1 Esdras 8:47 | Tobit 1:3*

78 And now in some measure hath mercy been shewed unto us from thee, O Lord, that there should be left us a root and a name in the place of thy sanctuary;

79 and to discover unto us a light in the house of the Lord our God, *and* to give us food in the time of our servitude.

80 Yea, when we were in bondage, we were not forsaken of our Lord; but he made us gracious before the kings of Persia, so that *they* gave us food;

81 *Yea*, and honoured the temple of our Lord, and raised up the desolate Sion, that *they* have given us a sure abiding in Jewry and Jerusalem.

Precept: Jewry = *The country of Judea, Judah: Daniel 5:13 | Luke 23:5 | John 7:1*

82 And now, O Lord, what shall we say, having these *things?* for we have transgressed thy commandments, which thou gavest by the hand of thy servants the prophets, saying,

83 that the land, which ye enter into to possess as an heritage, is a land polluted with the pollutions of the strangers of the land, and they have filled it with their uncleanness.

84 Therefore now shall ye not join your daughters unto their sons, neither shall ye take their daughters unto your sons.

85 Moreover ye shall never seek to have peace with them, that ye may be strong, and eat the good *things* of the land, and *that* ye may leave the inheritance *of the land* unto your children for evermore.

Precept: Inheritance = *Passing on of Land, portion of possessions that transfers to an heir upon the owner's physical death: Zechariah 9:2. 1) True inheritance cannot be stolen, brought, or transferred or outside the original owners inherent person:* **Revelation** *2:9;3:9 | Numbers 1:18 Transmission from parent to offspring. The acquisition of a possession, condition, or trait from past generations: Amos 3:1-2 | Psalm 147:19-20 2) Something that is inherited by heritage. 3) By birthright of the first born, imperishable heirloom of occupancy: Amos 3:1-2*

86 And all that is befallen is done unto us for our wicked works and great sins; for thou, O Lord, didst make our sins light,

87 and didst give unto us such a root: but we have turned back again to transgress thy law, *and* to mingle ourselves with the uncleanness of the nations of the land.

88 Mightest not thou be angry with us to destroy us, till *thou* hadst left us neither root, seed, nor name?

89 O Lord of Israel, thou art true: for we are left a root this day.

90 Behold, now are we before thee in our iniquities, for *we* cannot stand any longer by reason of these *things* before thee.

91 And as Esdras in his prayer made his confession, weeping, and lying flat upon the ground before the temple, there gathered unto him from Jerusalem a very great multitude *of* men and

women and children: for there was great weeping among the multitude.

Precept: Esdras = *Ez-druhs, is Greek. The Hebrew translation is Ezra* = *Ez-ruh; means: Yahawah is my help*

92 Then Jechonias *the son* of Jeelus, *one* of the sons of Israel, called out, and said, O Esdras, we have sinned against the Lord God, we have married strange women of the nations of the land, and now is all Israel aloft.

Precept: Nehemiah 13:27 | 1 King 11:8 | Ezra 10:2, 10 | Esdras = *Ez-druhs, is Greek. The Hebrew translation is Ezra* = *Ez-ruh; means: Yahawah is my help | Jechonias* = *JEK-oh-NIGH-uhs. They turn his name to Jehoiakim, and taken Jehoahaz away, means: Preparation, stability, of the Lord: 2 Kings 23:34 | Jeelus* = *Joh-EE-luhs | Israel* = *IZ-ray-el; means: A prince of God | Aloft* = *On high, Exalted: Deuteronomy 28:13 | Obadiah 4 | Sirach/Ecclesiasticus 34:1; 24:13 | Baruch 5:6 | Jeremiah 49*

93 Let us make an oath to the Lord, that *we* will put away all our wives, which *we have taken* of the heathen, with their children,

Precept: Heathen = *Gentiles: The Most High cast out before the children of Israel: 2 Kings 16:3 | The Isle: Genesis 10:5*

94 *like* as thou hast decreed, and as many as do obey the law of the Lord.

Precept: Decreed = *Ordinance, Resolved, Determined: 2 Chronicles 30:5 | Ezra 6:8 | Romans 13:2 | Numbers 15:15 | Judith 11:13 | Exodus 21:22 | 1 Samuel 20:7*

95 Arise and put in execution: for to thee doth *this* matter appertain, and we will be with thee: do valiantly.

Precept: Appertaineth/Appertain = *ap-er-tan; means: Only once, It becometh, It is seemly, pertain, and It is Thy honor: Jeremiah 10:7 | Leviticus 6:5 | Nehemiah 2:8 | Valiantly* = *Might, Valor, Mighty men, Mighty in war, Power, Powerful: Genesis 6:4 | Exodus 15:15 | Joshua 1:14 | Isaiah 3:25 | 1 Samuel 16:18 | Deuteronomy 4:34 | Sirach/Ecclesiasticus 46:1*

96 So Esdras arose, and took an oath of the chief of the priests and Levites of all Israel to do after these *things;* and so they sware.

Precept: Esdras = *Ez-druhs, is Greek. The Hebrew translation is Ezra* = *Ez-ruh; means: Yahawah is my help | Priests* = *Called Ministers*

1 ESDRAS CHAPTER 9

1 Then Esdras rising from the court of the temple went to the chamber of Joanan the *son* of Eliasib,
Precept: **Esdras** = *Ez-druhs, is Greek. The Hebrew translation is* **Ezra** = *Ez-ruh; means: Yahawah is my help* | **Joanan** = *joh-AY-nuhn* | **Eliasib** = *ih-LIGH-uh-sib*

2 and remained there, and did eat no meat nor drink water, mourning for the great iniquities of the multitude.

3 And there was a proclamation in all Jewry and Jerusalem to all them that were of the captivity, that *they* should be gathered together at Jerusalem:
Precept: **Proclamation** = *Public Announcement* | **Jewry** = *The country of Judea, Judah: Daniel 5:13* | *Luke 23:5* | *John 7:1*

4 and *that* whosoever met not *there* within two or three days according as the elders that bare rule appointed, their cattle should be seized to the use of the temple, and himself cast out from them that were of the captivity.
Precept: **Elders** = *Ancients of the Jews: 1 Esdras 6:5, 11, 27; 7:1* | *Exodus 3:16* | *Genesis 50:7* | *Numbers 11:16-17; 22:7* | *1 Samuel 24:13* | *Matthew 5:21*

5 And in three days were all they of the tribe of Judah and Benjamin gathered together at Jerusalem the twentieth day of the ninth month.
Precept: Ezra 10:9-44

6 And all the multitude sat trembling in the broad court of the temple because of the present foul weather.

7 So Esdras arose up, and said unto them, Ye have transgressed the law in marrying strange wives, *thereby* to increase the sins of Israel.
Precept: Ezra 10:18 | *Nehemiah 13:27* | **Esdras** = *Ez-druhs, is Greek. The Hebrew translation is* **Ezra** = *Ez-ruh; means: Yahawah is my help*

8 And now by confessing give glory unto the Lord God of our fathers,

9 and do his will, and separate yourselves from the heathen of the land, and from the strange women.

10 Then cried the whole multitude, and said with a loud voice, Like as thou hast spoken, *so* will we do.

11 But forasmuch as the people are many, and *it is* foul weather, so that we cannot stand without, and this is not a work of a day or two, seeing our sin in these *things* is spread far:

12 therefore let the rulers of the multitude stay, and let all them of our habitations that have strange wives come at the time appointed,

13 and *with them* the rulers and judges of every place, till we turn away the wrath of the Lord from us for this matter.

14 Then Jonathan *the son* of Azael and Ezechias *the son* of Theocanus accordingly took *this matter* upon *them*: and Mosollam and Levis and Sabbatheus helped them.

Precept: Jonathan = *JAHN-uh-thuhn; means: Yahawah has given* | **Azael** = *AY-zay-el. The Hebrew translation is* **Asahel** = *ASS-uh-hel; means: El has done: Ezra 10:15* | **Ezechias** = *ez-uh-KIGH-uhs. The Hebrew translation is* **Jahzeiah** = *jay-huh-ZIGH-uh; means: Yahawah sees, reveals:Ezra 10:15* | **Theocanus** = *thee-AHK-uh-muhs. The Hebrew translation is* **Tikvah** = *TIK-vah; means: Hope: Ezra 10:15* | **Mosollam** = *mot-SAHL-uhm* | **Levis** = *LEE-viss* | **Sabbatheus** = *sab-uh-THEE-uhs*

15 And they that were of the captivity did according to all these *things*.

16 And Esdras the priest chose unto him *the* principal men of their families, all by name: and in the first day of the tenth month they sat together to examine the matter.

Precept: Esdras = *Ez-druhs, is Greek. The Hebrew translation is* **Ezra** = *Ez-ruh;*

means: Yahawah is my help

17 So their cause that held strange wives was brought to an end in the first day of the first month.

18 And of the priests that were come together, and had strange wives, there were found:

19 Of the sons of Jesus the *son* of Josedec, and his brethren; Matthelas and Eleazar, and Joribus and Joadanus.
*Precept: **Josedec** = JAHS-uh-dek, or **Jozadak** = JAHZ-uh-dak; means: Yahawah acts in righteousness: 1 Chronicles 6:14-15 | Haggai 1:1 | Ezra 3:2 | **Joribus** = juh-RIGH-buhs. He is called **Jarib** = JAY-rib in Ezra 8:16; means: Strive, contend | **Yahawashi** or **Jesus** = YAH-how-WAH-shi | **Matthelas** = MATH-uh-luhs | **Eleazar** = EL-ih-AY-zuhr; means: God helps | **Joadanus** = joh-AD-uh-nuhs | **Brethren** = breth-ran: means: Referring to the members of a Sect, society, or of Profession. Many times used as Brother: Genesis 9:22, 25; 19:7 | Deuteronomy 3:20; 10:9 | 1 Esdras 8:47 | Tobit 1:3*

20 And they gave their hands to put away their wives and *to offer* rams to make reconcilement for their errors.

21 And of the sons of Emmer; Ananias, and Zabdeus, and Eanes, and Sameius, and Hiereel, and Azarias.
*Precept: **Emmer** = EM-uhr. The Hebrew translation is **Immer** = IM-uhr; means: Lamb: Ezra 2:37 | **Ananias** = uh-tehr-uh-ZIGH-uhs; means: Yahawah has dealt graciously | **Zabdeus** = ZAB-dee-uhs | **Eanes** = EE-uh-neez | **Sameius** = suh-MEE-yuhs | **Hiereel** = high-IHR-ee-el | **Azarias** = az-uh-RIGH-uhs*

22 And of the sons of Phaisur; Elionas, Massias Ismael, and Nathanael, and Ocidelus and Talsas.
*Precept: **Nathanael** = nut-THAN-ay-uhl; means: Gift of God | **Phaisur** = FAY-zuhr, is Egyptian; means: Son of Horus | **Elionas** = el-ih-OH-nuhs | **Massias** = muh-SIGH-uhs | **Ismael** = ISS-may-el | **Nathanael** = nut-THAN-ay-uhl; means: Gift of God | **Ocidelus** = oh-sigh-DIH-luhs | **Talsas** = TAL-suhs*

23 And of the Levites; Jozabad, and Semis, and Colius, who was *called* Calitas, and Patheus, and Judas, and Jonas.
*Precept: **Levites** = LEE-vi | **Jozabad** = JAHZ-uh-bad | **Semis** = SEE-miss | **Colius** = Koh-LIGH-uhs | **Calitas** = kuh-LIGHT-uhs | **Patheus** = puh-THEE-uhs | **Judas** = JOO-duhs | **Jonas** = JOH-nuhs*

24 Of the holy singers; Eleazurus, Bacchurus.

Precept: Eleazurus = *el-ih-uh-ZOOR-uhs* | *Bacchurus* = *ba-KYOOR-uhs*

25 Of the porters; Sallumus, and Tolbanes.

Precept: Sallumus = *SAL-uh-muhs* | *Tolbanes* = *TAHL-buh-neez*

26 Of *them of* Israel, of the sons of Phoros; Hiermas, and Eddias, and Melchias, and Maelus, and Eleazar, and Asibias, and Baanias.

Precept: Eleazar = *E-ih-AY-zuhr; means: God has helped* | *Israel* = *IZ-ray-el; means: A prince of God* | *Phoros* = *FAHR-ahs, is the same person named* *Parosh* = *PAY-rahsh: means: Flea* | *Hiermas* = *high-UHR-muhs* | *Eddias* = *ih-DIGH-uhs* | *Melchias* = *mel-KIGH-uhs* | *Maelus* = *MAY-uh-luhs* | *Asibias* = *ass-uh-BIGH-uhs* | *Baanias* = *bay-uh-NIGH-uhs*

27 Of the sons of Ela; Matthanias, Zacharias, and Hierielus, and Hieremoth, and Aedias.

Precept: Zacharias = *ZAK-uh-RIGH-uhs; means: Yahweh remembers* | *Ela* = *EE-luh* | *Matthanias* = *math-uh-NIGH-uhs* | *Hierielus* = *high-ihr-ih-EE-luhs* | *Hieremoth* = *high-IHR-uh-mahth* | *Aedias* = *a-e-di-AS*

28 And of the sons of Zamoth; Eliadas, Elisimus, Othonias, Jarimoth, and Sabatus, and Sardeus.

Precept: Zamoth =*ZAY-mahth* | *Eliadas* = *ih-LIGH-uh-duhs* | *Elisimus* = *ih-LISS-ih-muhs* | *Othonias* = *ahth-uh-NIGH-uhs* | *Jerimoth* = *JEHR-ih-mahth* | *Sabatus* = *SAB-uh-tuhs* | *Sardeus* = *sahr-DEE-uhs*

29 Of the sons of Bebai; Johannes, and Ananias and Josabad, and Amatheis.

Precept: Johannes = *John-HAN-iz* | *Josabad* = *JAHS=uh-bad; means: the LORD is a gift, or The LORD has given* | *Bebai* = *BEE-bigh* | *Ananias* = *an-uh-NIGH-uhs* | *Amatheis* = *am-uh-THEE-uhs*

30 Of the sons of Mani; Olamus, Mamuchus, Jedeus, Jasubus, Jasael, and Hieremoth.

Precept: Mani = *MAY-nigh* | *Olamus* = *OH-luh-muhs* | *Mamuchus* = *muh-MYOO-kuhs* | *Jedeus* = *JED-ih-uhs* | *Jasubus* = *juh-SOO-buhs* | *Jasael* = *JAY-say-el* | *Hieremoth* = *high-IHR-uh-mahth*

31 And of the sons of Addi; Naathus, and Moosias, Lacunus, and

Naidus, and Mathanias, and Sesthel, Balnuus, and Manasseas.
Precept: Addi = AD-igh | Naathus = NAY-uh-thuhs | Moosias = moh-uh-SIGH-uhs |
Lacunus = luh-KOO-nuhs | Naidus = NIGH-dihs | Mathanias = math-uh-NIGH-uhs |
Sesthel = SEHS-thuhl | Balnuus = BAL-noo-uhs | Manasseas = muh-NASS-ih-uhs

32 And of the sons of Annas; Elionas and Aseas, and Melchias, and Sabbeus, and Simon Chosameus.
Precept: Annas = AN-uhs; means: Merciful | Elionas = el-ih-OH-nuhs | Aseas = ASS-
ee-uhs | Melchias = mel-KIGH-uhs | Sabbeus = sa-BEE-uhs | Simon = SIGH-muhn |
Chosameeus = koh-suh-MEE-uhs

33 And of the sons of Asom; Altaneus, and Matthias, and Bannaia, Eliphalet, and Manasses, and Semei.
Precept: Eliphalet = ih-LIF-uh-let. The Hebrew translation is Eliphelet = ih-LIF-eh-
let; means: El [God] is deliverance, The divine deliverer: 1 Chronicles 3:6 | Asom =
AY-sahm | Altaneus = al-tuh-NEE-uhs | Matthias = muh-THIGH-uhs | Bannaia =
buh-NAY-yuh | Eliphalet = ih-LIF-uh-let. The Hebrew translation is Eliphelet = ih-
LIF-eh-let; means: El [God] is deliverance, The divine deliverer: 1 Chronicles 3:6 |
Manasses = muh-NASS-eez | Semei = SEM-ih-igh

34 And of the sons of Maani; Jeremias, Momdis, Omaerus, Juel, Mabdai, and Pelias, and Anos, Carabasion, and Enasibus, and Mamnitanaimus, Eliasis, Bannus, Eliali, Samis, Selemias, Nathanias: and of the sons of Ozora; Sesis, Esril, Azaelus, Samatus, Zambis, Josephus.
Precept: Maani = MAY-uh-nigh | Jeremias = her-ih-MIGH-uhs. The Hebrew
translation is Jeremiah; means: May Yahawah raise up | Momdis = MAHM-diss |
Omaerus = oh-MEE-ruhs | Juel = JOO-uhl | Mabdai = MAB-digh | Pelias = PEE-lih-
uhs | Anos = AY-nahs | Carabasion = kehr-uh-BAY-zhee-uhn | Enasibus = ih-NASS-
ih-buhs | Mamnitanaimus = MAM-ni-ta-ne-mus | Eliasis = ih-LIGH-uh-siss | Bannus
= BAN-uhs | Eliali = ih-LIGH-uh-ligh | Samis = SAY-miss | Selemias = sel-uh-MIGH-
uhs | Nathanias = nath-uh-NIGH-uhs | Ozora = oh-ZAWR-uh | Sesis = SEE-siss |
Esril = ES-rihl | Azaelus = az-uh-EE-luhs | Samatus = suh-MAY-tuhs | Zambis =
zam-bis | Josephus = joh-SEE-fuhs

35 And of the sons of Ethma; Mazitias, Zabadaias, Edes, Juel, Bannaia.
Precept: Ethma = ETH-muh | Mazitias = maz-uh-TIGH-uhs | Zabadaias = zab-a-da-
yas, His short name in Hebrew was Zabad = ZAY-bad; means: Yahawah has made a
gift: 1 Chronicles 2:36-37 | Edes = EE-deez | Juel = JOO-uhl | Bannaia = BAN-na-ia

36 All these had taken strange wives, and they put them away

with *their* children.

37 And the priests and Levites, and they that were of Israel, dwelt in Jerusalem, and in the country, in the first day of the seventh month: so the children of Israel were in their habitations.
Precept: Israel = IZ-ray-el; means: A prince of God

38 And the whole multitude came together with one accord into the broad place of the holy porch toward the east:

39 and they spake unto Esdras the priest and reader, that he would bring the law of Moses, that was given of the Lord God of Israel.
Precept: Esdras = Ez-druhs, is Greek. The Hebrew translation is Ezra = Ez-ruh; means: Yahawah is my help | Israel = IZ-ray-el; means: A prince of God

40 So Esdras the chief priest brought the law unto the whole multitude from man to woman, and to all the priests, to hear law in the first day of the seventh month.
Precept: Esdras = Ez-druhs, is Greek. The Hebrew translation is Ezra = Ez-ruh; means: Yahawah is my help

41 And he read in the broad court before the holy porch from morning unto midday, before both men and women; and the multitude gave heed unto the law.

42 And Esdras the priest and reader of the law stood up upon a pulpit of wood, which was made *for that purpose.*
Precept: Esdras = Ez-druhs, is Greek. The Hebrew translation is Ezra = Ez-ruh; means: Yahawah is my help

43 And there stood up by him Mattathias, Sammus, Ananias, Azarias, Urias, Ezecias, Balasamus, upon the right hand:
Precept: Mattathias = mat-uh-THIGH-uhs | Sammus = SAM-uhs | Ananias = uh-tehr-uh-ZIGH-uhs; means: Yahawah has dealt graciously | Azarias = az-uh-RIGH-uhs | Urias = yoo-RIGH-uhs | Ezecias = ez-uh-KIGH-uhs | Balasamus = buh-LASS-uh-muhs

44 and upon *his* left hand *stood* Phaldaius, Misael, Melchias, Lothasubus, and Nabarias.

Precept: Phaldaius = *fal-DAY-uhs* | *Misael* = *MISS-ay-el* | *Melchias* = *mel-KIGH-uhs* | *Lothausbus* = *loh-THAH-suh-buhs* | *Nabarias* = *nab-uh-RIGH-uhs*

45 Then took Esdras the book of the law before the multitude: for he sat honourably in the first place in the sight of *them* all.

Precept: Esdras = *Ez-druhs, is Greek. The Hebrew translation is* ***Ezra*** *= Ez-ruh; means: Yahawah is my help*

46 And when *he* opened the law, they stood all straight up. So Esdras blessed the Lord God most High, the God of hosts, Almighty.

Precept: Esdras = *Ez-druhs, is Greek. The Hebrew translation is* ***Ezra*** *= Ez-ruh; means: Yahawah is my help* | *Blessed* = *Knowledge of God, All things, Giving knowledge of, Works, The Heavenly Gift of Knowledge, give understanding and knowledge of Blessed* = *Hallowed, Joined to, Joined, Give, Joined together, Gave knowledge to, Commanded , Praised, Holy, Render, Named Bless* = *Worship, Give, will Give, Will give you, give us a, praise, Nehemiah 9:5* | *Genesis 1:22* | *Psalm 33:12* | *2 Esdras 13:24*

47 And all the people answered, Amen; and lifting up *their* hands they fell to the ground, and worshipped the Lord.

48 *Also* Jesus, Anus, Sarabias, Adinus, Jacubus, Sabateus, Auteas, Maianeas, and Calitas, Asrias, and Joazabdus, and Ananias, Biatas, the Levites, taught the law of the Lord, making them withal to understand it.

Precept: Yahawashi or Jesus = *YAH-how-WAH-shi* | *Anus* = *AY-nuhs* | *Sarabias* = *sehr-uh-BIGH-uhs* | *Adinus* = *uh-DIGH-nuhs* | *Jacubus* = *juh-KYOO-buhs* | *Sabateus* = *sab-a-TE-us* | *Auteas* = *aw-TEE-uhs* | *Maianeas* = *may-AN-ih-uhs* | *Calitas* = *kuh-LIGHT-uhs* | *Asrias* = *az-uh-RIGH-as* | *Joazabdus* = *joh-uh-ZAB-duhs* | *Ananias* = *uh-tehr-uh-ZIGH-uhs; means: Yahawah has dealt graciously* | *Biatas* = *BIGH-uh-tuhs*

49 Then spake Attharates unto Esdras the chief priest. and reader, and to the Levites that taught the multitude, even to all, saying,

Precept: Esdras = *Ez-druhs, is Greek. The Hebrew translation is* ***Ezra*** *= Ez-ruh; means: Yahawah is my help* | *Attharates* = *auth-uh-RAY-teez*

50 This day is holy unto the Lord; (for they all wept when *they* heard the law:)

51 go then, and eat the fat, and drink the sweet, and send part to them that have nothing;

52 for this day is holy unto the Lord: and be not sorrowful; for the Lord will bring you to honour.

53 So the Levites published all *things* to the people, saying, This day is holy to the Lord; be not sorrowful.

54 Then went they their way, every one to eat and drink, and make merry, and to give part to them that had nothing, and to make great cheer;

55 because they understood the words wherein they were instructed, and *for the which* they had been assembled.

2 ESDRAS

2 ESDRAS CHAPTER 1

1 The second book of the prophet Esdras, the son of Saraias, the son of Azarias, the son of Helchias, the son of Sadamias, the son of Sadoc, the son of Achitob,

Precept: Ezra 7:2 |1 Chronicles 6:12 | **Saraias** = such-RAY-yuhs; means: Yahawah has persevered or persisted | **Esdras** = Ez-druhs, is Greek. The Hebrew translation is **Ezra** = Ez-ruh; means: Yahawah is my help | **Achitob** = AK-uh-tahb, is Greek. The Hebrew translation is **Ahitub** = uh-HIGH-tuhb: 1 Samuel 14:3; 22:9 | **Azarias** = az-uh-RIGH-uhs | **Helchias** = HIL-Ki-isa | **Sadamias** = sad-uh-MIGH-uhs; means; The requited | **Sadoc** = SAY-dahk

2 the son of Achias, the son of Phinees, the son of Heli, the son of Amarias, the son of Aziei, the son of Marimoth, the son of Arna, the son of Ozias, the son of Borith, the son of Abisei, the son of Phinees, the son of Eleazar,

Precept: **Phinees** = Fin-ih-uhs is Greek. His Hebrew name is **Phinehas** = FIN-ih-huhs; means: Dark-skinned one. One of Ezra's progenitors: 2 Esdras 1:2. However, this link is not found in Ezra's genealogy checking 1 Esdras 8:1, Ezra 7:1, or 1 Chronicles chapter 6. this will be found in 2 Esdras 1:2, Ezra's descent was from Eleazar, while Phinees (Phinehas) was a direct descendant of Ithamar, the youngest son of Aaron | **Amarias** = am-uh-RIGH-uhs, is Greek. The Hebrew translation is **Amariah** = am-uh-RIGH-uh; means: The Lord has spoken, The lord has promised: 1 Chronicles 5:33-34; 6:37-37 | **Eleazar** = E-ih-AY-zuhr; means: God has helped | **Achias** = uh-KIGH-uhs | **Heli** = HEE-ligh; means:High | **Aziei** = az-uh-EE-igh | **Marimoth** = MAHR-ih-mahth | **Arna** = AHR-nuh | **Ozias** = oh-ZIGH-uhs, and in the Old aTestament the Name Uzziah = uh-ZIGH-uh; meaning: Yahawah is strong, mighty: 2 Kings 15:32 | **Borith** = BAHR-ith |**Abisei** = ab-uh-SEE-igh |

3 the son of Aaron, of the tribe of Levi; which was captive in the land of the Medes, in the reign of Artexerxes king of the Persians.

Precept: **Artexerxes** = ar-TAKS-urk'-sez | **Persians** = our-SHANZ: Country laying east of Mesopotamia (modern Iraq) | **Aaron** = EHR-uhn; means: Mountaineer, Enlightened | **Levi** = LEE-vigh; means: a joining | **Medes** = Me-di-a |

4 And the word of the Lord came unto me, saying,

5 Go *thy way*, and shew my people their sinful deeds, and their children *their* wickedness which they have done against me; that they may tell *their* children's children:

6 because the sins of their fathers are increased in them: for they have forgotten me, and have offered unto strange gods.

7 *Am* not I even *he that* brought them out of the land of Egypt, from the house of bondage? but they have provoked me unto wrath, and despised my counsels.

8 Pull thou off then the hair of thy head, and cast all evil upon them, for they have not been obedient unto my law, but it is a rebellious people.
Precept: Rebellious = *Resistance, Rebellion, Opposition to authority, Disobedient, Rebelled: Joshua 22:22 | 1 Samuel 15:23 | Job 34:37 | Jeremiah 28:16; 29:32 | 1 Esdras 2:27*

9 How long shall I forbear them, into whom I have done so much good?
Precept: Numbers 14:11

10 Many kings have I destroyed for their sakes; Pharaoh with his servants and all his power have I smitten down.

11 All the nations have I destroyed before them, and in the east I have scattered the people of two provinces, *even* of Tyrus and Sidon, and have slain all their enemies.
Precept: Tyrus = *TIGH-ruhs: An ancient towns Phoenician coast | Sidon = SIGH-duhn: The city of ancient Phoencia. Situated on the E Mediterranean coast about 25 miles N of Tyre, Sidon.*

12 Speak thou therefore unto them, saying, Thus saith the Lord,

13 I led you through the sea and in the beginning gave you a large and safe passage; I gave you Moses *for* a leader, and Aaron *for* a priest.

14 I gave you light in a pillar of fire, and great wonders have I done among you; yet have ye forgotten me, saith the Lord.

15 Thus saith the Almighty Lord, The quails were as a token to you; I gave you tents for *your* safeguard: nevertheless ye murmured there,
Precept: Exodus 16:13

16 and triumphed not in my name for the destruction of your enemies, but ever to this day do ye yet murmur.

17 Where are the benefits that I have done for you? when ye were hungry *and thirsty* in the wilderness, did ye not cry unto me,

18 Saying, Why hast thou brought us into this wilderness to kill us? it had been better for us to have served the Egyptians, than to die in this wilderness.
Precept: Numbers 14:3 | Exodus 14:12

19 Then had I pity upon your mournings, and gave you manna to eat; *so* ye did eat angels' bread.
*Precept: Wisdom 16:20 | Exodus 16:14-15 | **Angel** = appear in a dream is a spirit angel. And angel appear in the flesh is an messenger of the flesh (A Nazarite, vowed to God, many times) of God: Matthew 2:13, 19 in a dream | Genesis 31:11*

20 When ye were thirsty, did I not cleave the rock, and waters flowed *out* to your fill? for the heat I covered you with the leaves of the trees.
Precept: Wisdom 11:4

21 I divided among you a fruitful land, I cast out the Canaanites, the Pherezites, and the Philistines, before you: what shall I yet do more for you? saith the Lord.
*Precept: Exodus 3:8 | Isaiah 5:4 | **Canaanites** = KAY-nuhn-ight | **Pherezites** = Fer-e-SITES | **Philistines** = FIL-lis-teenz |*

22 Thus saith the Almighty Lord, When ye were in the wilderness, in the river of the Amorites, being athirst, and blaspheming my name,

Precept: Canaanites = KAY-nuhn-ight | Athirst = suffering from thirst | Amorites = AM-uh-right; means: To see, to provide | Blaspheming = False witness spoken against one | Wilfull contradiction of the truth: Numbers 21:7 | Ezekiel 35:12 | Jude 15

23 I gave you not fire for *your* blasphemies, but cast a tree in the water, and made the river sweet.

Precept: Exodus 15:25 | Sirach/Ecclesiasticus 38:5 | Blaspheming = False witness spoken against one | Wilfull contradiction of the truth: Numbers 21:7 | Ezekiel 35:12 | Jude 15

24 What shall I do unto thee, O Jacob? thou, Juda, wouldest not obey *me*: I will turn me to other nations, and unto those will I give my name, that they may keep my statutes.

Precept: Jacob = KAY-nuhn-ight | Joda = JOH-duh, is the same Juda = JOO-duh

25 Seeing ye have forsaken me, I will forsake you also; when ye desire me to be gracious unto you, I shall have no mercy *upon you.*

Precept: Leviticus 26:23-24 | Psalms 37:13; 59:8 | Proverbs 1:26 | 2 Chronicles 15:2; 24:20 | Jeremiah 23:33, 39

26 Whensoever ye shall call upon me, I will not hear you: for ye have defiled your hands with blood, and your feet are swift to commit manslaughter.

Precept: Proverbs 1:28 | Isaiah 59:7

27 Ye have not as it were forsaken me, but your own selves, saith the Lord.

28 Thus saith the Almighty Lord, Have I not prayed you as a father *his* sons, as a mother *her* daughters, and a nurse her young babes,

29 that ye would be my people, and I *should be* your God; that ye

would be my children, and I *should be* your father?

30 I gathered you together, as a hen *gathereth* her chickens under her wings: but now, what shall I do unto you? I will cast you out from my face.
Precept: *Matthew 23:37 | Luke 13:34*

31 When ye offer unto me, I will turn my face from you: for your solemn feastdays, *your* new moons, and *your* circumcisions, have I forsaken.
Precept: *Isaiah 1:13-14*

32 I sent unto you my servants the prophets, whom ye have taken and slain, and torn their bodies in pieces, whose blood I will require *of your hands,* saith the Lord.
Precept: *2 Chronicles 36:15-16 | Jeremiah 7:25; 26:5; 29;19; 35:15; 44:4 |* **Prophets** *= A prophet of God is one who has authority and who has the qualifications to convey God's messages to men. Being God's mouth piece. A prophet interpret scripture Parables, Riddles, and dark speeches, giving one the Oracles and the mystery of God word: Jeremiah 3:15; 44:4 | 2 Kings 17:13 | 1 Chronicles 16:22 | Psalms 105:15 | 2 Esdras 1:32 | Matthew 13:35*

33 Thus saith the Almighty Lord, Your house is desolate, I will cast you out as the wind *doth* stubble.
Precept: *Matthew 23:38 | Luke 13:35 | Leviticus 20:23 | Nehemiah 1:9 | Jeremiah 7:15 | Job 21:18 | Psalm 83:13 | Isaiah 40:24*

34 And *your* children shall not be fruitful; for they have despised my commandment, and done *the thing* that *is* an evil before me.
Precept: *Deuteronomy 28:18 | Romans 9:8*

35 Your houses will I give to a people that shall come; which not having heard *of* me yet shall believe *me;* to whom I have shewed no signs, *yet* they shall do that I have commanded *them.*

36 They have seen no prophets, yet they shall call their sins to remembrance, *and acknowledge them.*
Precept: *Hebrews 10:2-3 | 1 Kings 17:18 |* **Prophets** *= A prophet of God is one who has authority and who has the qualifications to convey God's messages to men. Being*

82

God's mouth piece. A prophet interpret scripture Parables, Riddles, and dark speeches, giving one the Oracles and the mystery of God word: Jeremiah 3:15; 44:4 | 2 Kings 17:13 | 1 Chronicles 16:22 | Psalms 105:15 | 2 Esdras 1:32 | Matthew 13:35

37 I take to witness the grace of the people to come, whose little ones rejoice in gladness: and though they have not seen me with bodily eyes, yet in spirit they believe *the thing* that I say.

38 And now, brother, behold what glory; and see the people that come from the east:
Precept: *Matthew 8:11*

39 unto whom I will give for leaders, Abraham, Isaac, and Jacob, Oseas, Amos, and Micheas, Joel, Abdias, and Jonas,
Precept: Jonas = *JOH-nuhs* | **Abraham** = *AY-bruh-ham; means: Father of a multitude* | **Isaac** = *IGH-zik; means: Laughter* | **Jacob** = *JAY-kuhb; means: Supplants* | **Oseas** = *oh-SEE-uhs, is Greek. The Hebrew translation is Hoshea = how-SHEE-uh; means: Salvation: Numbers 13:8 | Deuteronomy 32:44* | **Micheas** = *MIK-ih-uhs* | **Joel** = *JOH-el* | **Abdias** = *ab-DIGH-uhs* | **Jonas** = *JOH-nuhs*

40 Nahum, and Abacuc, Sophonias, Aggeus, Zacharie, and Malachie, which is called also an angel of the Lord.
Precept: Aggeus = *AG-ee-uhs, is Greek. His name in Hebrew is* **Haggai** = *HAG-igh: Haggai 1:1* | **Nahum** = *NAY-hoom* | **Abacuc** = *AB-uh-kuhk* | **Sophonias** = *sahf-uh-NIGH-uhs* | **Angel** = *appear in a dream is a spirit angel. And angel appear in the flesh is an messenger of the flesh (A Nazarite, vowed to God, many times) of God: Matthew 2:13, 19 in a dream | Genesis 31:11*

2 ESDRAS CHAPTER 2

1 Thus saith the Lord, I brought this people out of bondage, and I gave them *my* commandments by menservants the prophets; whom they would not hear, but despised my counsels.
*Precept: Proverbs 1:30 | 2 Esdras 1:7 | **Prophet** = A prophet of God is one who has authority and who has the qualifications to convey God's messages to men. Being God's mouth piece. A prophet interpret scripture Parables, Riddles, and dark speeches, giving one the Oracles and the mystery of God word: Jeremiah 3:15; 44:4 | 2 Kings 17:13 | 1 Chronicles 16:22 | Psalms 105:15 | 2 Esdras 1:32 | Matthew 13:35*

2 The mother that bare them saith unto them, Go *your way*, ye children; for I am a widow and forsaken.
Precept: Isaiah 47:8

3 I brought you up with gladness; but with sorrow and heaviness have I lost you: for ye have sinned before the Lord your God, and done *that thing* that is evil before him.
Precept: Tobit 13:6 | 1 Kings 16:25, 30

4 But what shall I now do unto you? I am a widow and forsaken: go *your way*, O *my* children, and ask mercy of the Lord.
Precept: Isaiah 47:8

5 As for me, O father, I call upon thee *for* a witness over the mother of these children, which would not keep my covenant,

6 that thou bring them to confusion, and their mother to a spoil, that there may be no offspring of them.
Precept: 2 Esdras 1:34

7 Let them be scattered abroad among the heathen, let their names be put out of the earth: for they have despised my covenant.
Precept: Ezekiel 12:15; 20:23; 36:19 | Deuteronomy 32:26 | 1 Kings 14:15 | Jeremiah 9:16 | Zechariah 7:14 | Tobit 13:3 | Baruch 2:29 | Matthew 9:36

8 Woe be unto thee, Assur, *thou* that hidest the unrighteous in

thee! O thou wicked people, remember what I did unto Sodom and Gomorrha;

*Precept: Genesis 10:11-12 | Psalm 83:8 | **Assur** = ASS-uhr | **Sodom** = SAHD-uhm | **Gomorrah** = guh-MAHR-uh; means: Land of Iniquity (Sin)*

9 whose land lieth in clods of pitch and heaps of ashes: *even* so *also* will I do unto them that hear me not, saith the Almighty Lord.

*Precept: **Clods** = Crust: Genesis 19:24 | Isaiah 28:24 | Hosea 10:11*

10 Thus saith the Lord unto Esdras, Tell my people that I will give them the kingdom of Jerusalem, which I would have given unto Israel.

*Precept: **Esdras** = Ez-druhs, is Greek. The Hebrew translation is **Ezra** = Ez-ruh; means: Yahawah is my help | **Israel** = IZ-ray-el; means: A prince of God*

11 Their glory also will I take unto me, and give these the everlasting tabernacles, which I had prepared for them.

12 They shall have the tree of life for an ointment of sweet savour; they shall neither labour, nor be weary.

Precept: Isaiah 5:27

13 Go, and ye shall receive: pray for few days unto you, that they may be shortened: the kingdom is already prepared for you: watch.

Precept: Matthew 24:22 | Mark 13:20 | Job 17:1

14 Take heaven and earth to witness; for I have broken the evil in pieces, and created the good: for I live, saith the Lord.

*Precept: Deuteronomy 4:26; 30:19; 31:28 | Judith 7:28 | 1 Maccabees 2:37 | **Heaven** = Firmament Separated from he earth. The color blue of the sky was attributed to the chaotic waters that the firmament is separated: Genesis 1:7 | Deuteronomy 5:8 | Job 26:11 | 2 Samuel 22:8*

15 Mother, embrace thy children, *and* bring them up with gladness, make their feet as fast as a pillar: for I have chosen thee, saith the Lord.

Precept: Isaiah 41:9; 44:2

16 And those that be dead will I raise up again from their places, and bring them out of the graves: for I have known my name in Israel.
Precept: Daniel 12:2 | Ezekiel 37:12-13 | John 5:28-29; 6:39; 12:17 | **Israel** *= IZ-ray-el; means: A prince of God*

17 Fear not, thou mother of the children: for I have chosen thee, saith the Lord.
Precept: Isaiah 41:9; 44:2; 48:10 | Haggai 2:23

18 *For* thy help will I send my servants Esay and Jeremy, after whose counsel I have sanctified and prepared for thee twelve trees laden with divers fruits,
Precept: 1 Kings 20:6 | Jeremiah 7:25; 26:5; 35:15; 44:4 | 2 Esdras 1:32

19 and as many fountains flowing *with* milk and honey, and seven mighty mountains, whereupon there grow roses and lilies, whereby I will fill thy children with joy.
Precept: Exodus 3:8 | Numbers 16:14 | Deuteronomy 26:9; 27:3 | Jeremiah 11:5; 32:22 | Ezekiel 20:6 | Baruch 1:20 | 2 Esdras 5:24

20 Do right to the widow, judge for the fatherless, give to the poor, defend the orphan, clothe the naked,
Precept: Exodus 22:22 | Isaiah 1:17 Psalm 10:18; 82:3 | Isaiah 58:7 | 2 Chronicles 28:15 | Tobit 1:17

21 heal the broken and the weak, laugh not a lame *man* to scorn, defend the maimed, and let the blind *man* come into the sight of my clearness.
Precept: Leviticus 19:14 | Deuteronomy 27:18 | Esther 14:11 | Sirach/Ecclesiasticus 20:17; 30:10 | Matthew 9:24

22 Keep the old and young within thy walls.

23 Wheresoever thou findest the dead, take *them* and bury *them*, and I will give thee the first place in my resurrection.
Precept: Tobit 1:17-18

24 Abide still, O my people, and take thy rest, for thy quietness still come.

25 Nourish thy children, O *thou* good nurse; stablish their feet.

26 As *for* the servants whom I have given thee, there shall not one of them perish; for I will require them from among thy number.
Precept: John 17:12

27 Be not weary: for when the day of trouble and heaviness cometh, others shall weep and be sorrowful, but thou shalt be merry and have abundance.

28 The heathen shall envy *thee*, but they shall be able to do nothing against thee, saith the Lord.
Precept: Isaiah 54:17

29 My hands shall cover thee, so that thy children shall not see hell.
Precept: Exodus 33:22 | Psalm 91:4 | Isaiah 51:16 | Psalm 89:48 | John 8:51 | Matthew 16:28 | Luke 9:27

30 Be joyful, O *thou* mother, with thy children; for I will deliver thee, saith the Lord.

31 Remember thy children that sleep, for I shall bring them out of the sides of the earth, and shew mercy unto them: for I am merciful, saith the Lord Almighty.
Precept: 1 Thessalonians 4:14

32 Embrace thy children until I come and shew mercy unto them: for my wells run over, and my grace shall not fail.

33 I Esdras received a charge of the Lord upon the mount Oreb, that I should go unto Israel; but when I came unto them, they set

me at nought, and despised the commandment of the Lord.
Precept: Exodus 3:1 | Deuteronomy 4:10, 15 | Sirach/Ecclesiasticus 48:7 | Numbers 15:31 | Amos 2:4 | Esdras = Ez-druhs, is Greek. The Hebrew translation is Ezra = Ez-ruh; means: Yahawah is my help | Israel = IZ-ray-el; means: A prince of God | Oreb = OH-reb

34 And therefore I say unto you, O ye heathen, that hear and understand, look for your Shepherd, he shall give you everlasting rest; for he is nigh at hand, that shall come in the end of the world.
Precept: Matthew 11:29

35 Be ready to the reward of the kingdom, for the everlasting light shall shine upon you for evermore.
Precept: Isaiah 60:19-20 | Revelation 21:23

36 Flee the shadow of this world, receive the joyfulness of your glory: I testify my Saviour openly.
Precept: Acts 26:26 | Jeremiah 34:15

37 O receive the gift that is given *you*, and be glad, giving thanks unto him that hath led you to the heavenly kingdom.
Precept: 1 Thessalonians 2:12 | Heaven = Firmament Separated from he earth. The color blue of the sky was attributed to the chaotic waters that the firmament is separated: Genesis 1:7 | Deuteronomy 5:8 | Job 26:11 | 2 Samuel 22:8

38 Arise up and stand, behold the number of those that be sealed in the feast of the Lord;
Precept: Revelation 7:3-8 | Jeremiah 32:14 | Nehemiah 10:1

39 which are departed from the shadow of the world, *and* have received glorious garments of the Lord.
Precept: Wisdom 5:16

40 Take thy number, O Sion, and shut up those of thine that are clothed in white, which have fulfilled the law of the Lord.
Precept: Revelation 3:4

41 The number of thy children, whom thou longedst for, is

fulfilled: beseech the power of the Lord, that thy people, which have been called from the beginning, may be hallowed.
Precept: Ephesians 1:4

42 I Esdras saw upon the mount Sion a great people, whom I could not number, and they all praised the Lord with songs.
Precept: Revelation 7:9 | ***Esdras*** *= Ez-druhs, is Greek. The Hebrew translation is* ***Ezra*** *= Ez-ruh; means: Yahawah is my help*

43 And in the midst of them there was a young man of a high stature, taller than all the rest, and upon every one of their heads he set crowns, and was more exalted; which I marvelled at greatly.
Precept: Revelation 5:6–9 | ***Aloft*** *= On high, Exalted: Deuteronomy 28:13* | *Obadiah 4* | *Sirach/Ecclesiasticus 34:1; 24:13* | *Baruch 5:6* | *Jeremiah 49:22*

44 So I asked the angel, and said, Sir, what are these?
Precept: Revelation 7:14 | ***Angel*** *= appear in a dream is a spirit angel. And angel appear in the flesh is an messenger of the flesh (A Nazarite, vowed to God, many times) of God: Matthew 2:13, 19 in a dream* | *Genesis 31:11*

45 He answered and said unto me, These be they that have put off the mortal clothing, and put on the immortal, and have confessed the name of God: now are they crowned, and receive palms.
Precept: Revelation 2:10; 4:4

46 Then said I unto the angel, What young person is it that crowneth them, and giveth *them* palms in *their* hands?
Precept: Angel *= appear in a dream is a spirit angel. And angel appear in the flesh is an messenger of the flesh (A Nazarite, vowed to God, many times) of God: Matthew 2:13, 19 in a dream* | *Genesis 31:11*

47 So he answered and said unto me, It is the Son of God, whom they have confessed in the world. Then began I greatly to commend them that stood *so* stiffly for the name of the Lord.
Precept: Zechariah 3:8

48 Then the angel said unto me, Go *thy way*, and tell my people

what manner of *things*, and how great wonders of the Lord *thy* God, thou hast seen.

Precept: Angel = appear in a dream is a spirit angel. And angel appear in the flesh is an messenger of the flesh (A Nazarite, vowed to God, many times) of God: Matthew 2:13, 19 in a dream | Genesis 31:11

2 ESDRAS CHAPTER 3

1 In the thirtieth year after the ruin of the city I was in Babylon, and lay troubled upon my bed, and my thoughts came up over my heart:
*Precept: Luke 24:38 | **Babylon** = Confuse, Confound; An enormously important city in antiquity ("gate of the god")*

2 for I saw the desolation of Sion, and the wealth of them that dwelt at Babylon.
*Precept: **Babylon** = Confuse, Confound; An enormously important city in antiquity ("gate of the god") | **Desolation** = DES-O-lation = Loneliness, Sadness, Devastation, Ruin. Also called **Desolate**: Genesis 47:19 | Leviticus 26:34-35 | Isaiah 13:9 | 1 Esdras 1:58; 2:23*

3 And my spirit was sore moved, so that I began to speak words full of fear to the most High, and said,

4 O Lord, who bearest rule, thou spakest at the beginning, when thou didst plant the earth, and that *thyself* alone, and commandedst the people,

5 And gavest a body unto Adam without soul, which was the workmanship of thine hands, and didst breathe into him the breath of life, and he was made living before thee.
*Precept: Genesis 2:7 | **Adam** = Mankind*

6 And thou leadest him into paradise, which thy right hand had planted, before ever the earth came forward.
Precept: Genesis 2:8

7 And unto him thou gavest commandment to love thy way: which he transgressed, and immediately thou appointedst death in him and in his generations, of whom came nations, tribes, people, and kindreds, out of number.
Precept: Genesis 3:19

8 And every people walked after their own will, and did wonderful *things* before thee, and despised thy commandments.
Precept: Genesis 6:11-12

9 And again in process of time thou broughtest the flood upon those that dwelt in the world, and destroyedst them.
Precept: Genesis 7:10

10 And it came to pass in every of them, that as death *was* to Adam, so *was* the flood to these.
Precept: Revelation 12:15-16 | 2 Peter 2:5

11 Nevertheless one of them thou leftest, namely, Noah with his household, of whom *came* all righteous *men.*
Precept: Genesis 8:1 | 1 Peter 3:20

12 And it happened, that when they that dwelt upon the earth began to multiply, and had gotten them many children, and were a great people, they began again to be more ungodly than the first.

13 Now when they lived *so* wickedly before thee, thou didst choose thee a man from among them, whose name was Abraham.
Precept: Genesis 12:1; 17:5 | Abraham = AY-bruh-ham; means: Father of a multitude

14 Him thou lovedst, and unto him only thou shewedst thy will:
Precept: 2 Chronicles 20:7

15 and madest an everlasting covenant with him, promising him that thou wouldest never forsake his seed.
Precept: Genesis 17:7

16 And unto him thou gavest Isaac, and unto Isaac *also* thou gavest Jacob and Esau. As *for* Jacob, thou didst choose *him* to thee, and put by Esau: and *so* Jacob became a great multitude.
Precept: Genesis 21:2-3 | Genesis 25:25-26 | Malachi 1:2-3 | Romans 9:13 | Genesis 32:10 | Esau = EE-saw; means: Hairy | Isaac = IGH-zik; means: Laughter | Jacob =

JAY-kuhb; means: Supplants

17 And it came to pass, *that* when thou leadest his seed out of Egypt, thou broughtest *them* up to the mount Sinai.
Precept: Exodus 19:1

18 And bowing the heavens, thou didst set fast the earth, movedst the whole *world*, and madest the depths to tremble, and troubledst the *men of that* age.
*Precept: 2 Samuel 22:10 | Psalm 18:9; 144;5 | Philippians 2:10 | **Heaven** = Firmament Separated from he earth. The color blue of the sky was attributed to the chaotic waters that the firmament is separated: Genesis 1:7 | Deuteronomy 5:8 | Job 26:11 | 2 Samuel 22:8*

19 And thy glory went through four gates, of fire, and of earthquake, and of wind, and of cold; that thou mightest give the law unto the seed of Jacob, and diligence unto the generation of Israel.
*Precept: Exodus 19:16-18 | **Israel** = IZ-ray-el; means: A prince of God*

20 And *yet* tookest thou not away from them a wicked heart, that thy law might bring forth fruit in them.

21 For the first Adam bearing a wicked heart transgressed, and was overcome; and so *be* all *they* that are born of him.
*Precept: 2 Esdras 7:48 | **Adam** = Mankind*

22 Thus infirmity was made permanent; and the law *also* in the heart of the people with the malignity of the root; so that the good departed away, and the evil abode *still*.
Precept: Romans 7:8-13

23 So the times passed away, and the years were brought to an end: then didst thou raise thee up a servant, called David:
*Precept: **David** = DAY-vid. The name David is a suggested title to the throne, not a personal name; means: The True Messiah*

24 whom thou commandedst to build a city unto thy name, and

to offer incense and oblations unto thee therein.
Precept: 2 Samuel 7:5, 13

25 When this was done many years, then they that inhabited the city forsook *thee*,

26 and in all *things* did even as Adam and all his generations had done: for they also had a wicked heart:

27 and so thou gavest thy city over into the hands of thine enemies.
Precept: Adam = Mankind

28 Are their deeds then any better that inhabit Babylon, that they should therefore have the dominion over Sion?
Precept: Babylon = Confuse, Confound; An enormously important city in antiquity ("gate of the god")

29 For when I came thither, and had seen impieties without number, then my soul saw many evildoers in this thirtieth year, so that my heart failed me.
Precept: Psalm 73:26

30 For I have seen how thou sufferest them sinning, and hast spared wicked doers: and hast destroyed thy people, and hast preserved thine enemies, and hast not signified *it*.

31 I do not remember how this way may be left: Are they then of Babylon better than they of Sion?
Precept: Babylon = Confuse, Confound; An enormously important city in antiquity ("gate of the god")

32 Or *is there* any other people *that* knoweth thee beside Israel? or what generation hath so believed thy covenants as Jacob?
Precept: Israel = IZ-ray-el; means: A prince of God | Jacob = JAY-kuhb; means: Supplants

33 And yet their reward appeareth not, and *their* labour hath no

fruit: for I have gone here and there through the heathen, and I see that they flow in wealth, and think not upon thy commandments.

34 Weigh thou therefore our wickedness now in the balance, and their's *also* that dwell the world; and *so* shall thy name no where be found but in Israel.

Precept: Israel = *IZ-ray-el; means: A prince of God*

35 Or when *was it that* they which dwell upon the earth have not sinned in thy sight? or what people have so kept thy commandments?

36 Thou shalt find that Israel by name hath kept thy precepts; but not the heathen.

Precept: Israel = *IZ-ray-el; means: A prince of God*

2 ESDRAS CHAPTER 4

1 And the angel that was sent unto me, whose name was Uriel, gave me an answer,
*Precept: **Uriel** = YOO-rih-el, also known as YOOR-ee-uhl. A prominent Kohathite Levite who helped bring the ark from the home of Obed-edom to Jerusalem; 1 Chronicles 6:24; 15:5, 11 | **Angel** = appear in a dream is a spirit angel. And angel appear in the flesh is an messenger of the flesh (A Nazarite, vowed to God, many times) of God: Matthew 2:13, 19 in a dream | Genesis 31:11*

2 and said, Thy heart hath gone to far in this world, and thinkest thou to comprehend the way of the most High?
*Precept: 2 Esdras 5:34 | **Comprehend** = Understand: Job 37:5 | Isaiah 44:18 | Sirach/ Ecclesiasticus 32:8*

3 Then said I, Yea, my lord. And he answered me, and said, I am sent to shew thee three ways, and to set forth three similitudes before thee:
*Precept: **Similitude(s)** = Likeness, Resemblance; Likeness in nature or in appearance: Numbers 12:8 | Deuteronomy 4:12, 15-16 | Psalm 106:20 | Daniel 10:16 | Hosea 12:10*

4 whereof if thou canst declare me one, I will shew thee also the way that thou desirest to see, and I shall shew thee from whence the wicked heart cometh.

5 And I said, Tell *on*, my lord. Then said he unto me, Go *thy way*, weigh me the weight of the fire, or measure me the blast of the wind, or call me again the day that is past.

6 Then answered I and said, What man is able to do *that*, that thou shouldest ask such things of me?

7 And he said unto me, If I should ask thee how great dwellings are in the midst of the sea, or how many springs are in the beginning of the deep, or how many springs are above the firmament, or which are the outgoings of paradise:
*Precept: Proverbs 23:34 | Genesis 13:6, 12; 27:39 | Deuteronomy 33:28 | **Firmament** = Heaven; Firmament Separated from he earth. The color blue of the sky was*

attributed to the chaotic waters that the firmament is separated: Genesis 1:7 | Deuteronomy 5:8 | Job 26:11 | 2 Samuel 22:8

8 peradventure thou wouldest say unto me, I never went down into the deep, nor as yet into hell, neither did I ever climb up into heaven.

*Precept: Heaven = Firmament Separated from he earth. The color blue of the sky was attributed to the chaotic waters that the firmament is separated: Genesis 1:7 | Deuteronomy 5:8 | Job 26:11 | 2 Samuel 22:8 | **Peradventure** = PEAR-uh-vent-ture; Haply; Perhaps, possibly, Maybe: Genesis 18:24; 42:4 | Exodus 32:30 | Joshua 9:7*

9 Nevertheless now have I asked thee but only of the fire and wind, and *of* the day wherethrough thou hast passed, and *of things* from which thou canst not be separated, and *yet* canst thou give me no answer of them.

10 He said moreover unto me, Thine own *things*, and such as are grown up with thee, canst thou not know;

11 how should thy vessel then be able to comprehend the way of the Highest, and, the world being now outwardly corrupted to understand the corruption that is evident in my sight?

*Precept: Comprehend = Understand: Job 37:5 | Isaiah 44:18 | Sirach/Ecclesiasticus 32:8 | **Corruption** = Decay, Decomposition, Sinfulness, Decay life: Isaiah 1:4 | Leviticus 22:24-25 | Psalm 14:1 | Jeremiah 6:28 | Wisdom 14:12, 25 | Sirach/ Ecclesiasticus 28:6; 31:5*

12 Then said I unto him, It were better that we were not *at all*, than that we should live still in wickedness, and to suffer, and not to know wherefore.

13 He answered me, and said, I went into a forest into a plain, and the trees took counsel,

Precept: Judges 9:8 | 2 Chronicles 25:18

14 and said, Come, let us go and make war against the sea that it may depart away before us, and that we may make us more woods.

15 The floods of the sea also in like manner took counsel, and said, Come, let us go up and subdue the woods of the plain, that there also we may make us another country.

16 The thought of the wood was in vain, for the fire came and consumed it.

17 The thought of the floods of the sea *came* likewise *to nought*, for the sand stood *up* and stopped them.

18 If thou wert judge now betwixt these *two*, whom wouldest thou begin to justify? or whom wouldest thou condemn?

19 I answered and said, Verily *it is* a foolish thought *that* they *both* have devised, for the ground is given unto the wood, and the sea *also hath his* place to bear his floods.

20 Then answered he me, and said, Thou hast given a right judgment, but why judgest thou not thyself also?

21 For like as the ground is given unto the wood, and the sea to his floods: *even* so they that dwell upon the earth may understand nothing but *that* which is upon the earth: and he *that dwelleth* above the heavens *may only understand the things* that are above the height of the heavens.

Precept: Heaven = *Firmament Separated from he earth. The color blue of the sky was attributed to the chaotic waters that the firmament is separated: Genesis 1:7 | Deuteronomy 5:8 | Job 26:11 | 2 Samuel 22:8*

22 Then answered I and said, I beseech thee, O Lord, let me have understanding:

23 for it was not my mind to be curious of the high *things*, but of such as pass by us daily, *namely*, wherefore Israel is given up as a reproach to the heathen, *and for what cause* the people whom

thou hast loved is given over unto ungodly nations, and *why* the law of our forefathers is brought to nought, and the written covenants come to none effect,

Precept: Israel = IZ-ray-el; means: A prince of God

24 and we pass away out of the world as grasshoppers, and our life *is* astonishment and fear, and we are not worthy to obtain mercy.

25 What will he then do unto his name whereby we are called? of these *things* have I asked.

26 Then answered he me, and said, The more thou searchest, the more thou shalt marvel; for the world hasteth fast to pass away,

Precept: 1 John 2:17

27 and cannot comprehend *the things* that are promised to the righteous in time to come: for this world is full of unrighteousness and infirmities.

Precept: Comprehend = Understand: Job 37:5 | Isaiah 44:18 | Sirach/Ecclesiasticus 32:8 | Exodus 19:5 | 1 John 5:19

28 But as concerning *the things* whereof thou askest *me*, I will tell *thee*; for the evil is sown, but the destruction thereof is not yet come.

29 If therefore *that* which is sown be not turned upside down, and *if* the place where the evil is sown pass *not* away, *then* cannot it come that is sown *with* good.

30 For the grain of evil seed hath been sown in the heart of Adam from the beginning, and how much ungodliness hath it brought up unto this time? and *how much* shall it *yet* bring forth until the time of threshing come?

Precept: Adam = Mankind | Jeremiah 51:33 | Ungodliness = Characteristic of being wicked, or no fear of the God of Israel: Psalm 36:1 Jude 15-16, 18 | Wisdom 14:9 | Romans 11:26 | 2 Timothy 2:16

31 Ponder now by thyself, how great fruit of wickedness the grain of evil seed hath brought forth.
Precept: *2 Thessalonians 2:3 | John 17:12 | Philippians 1:28 | 2 Peter 3:7 |*

32 *And* when the ears shall be cut down, which are without number, how great a floor shall they fill?

33 Then I answered and said, How, and when shall these *things come to pass?* wherefore *are* our years few and evil?

34 And he answered me, saying, Do not thou hasten above the most High*est*: for thy haste is in vain to be above him, for thou hast much exceeded.

35 Did not the souls *also* of the righteous ask question of these *things* in their chambers, saying, How long shall I hope on this fashion? when cometh the fruit of the floor of our reward?

36 And unto these *things* Uriel the archangel gave *them* answer, and said, *Even* when the number of seeds is filled in you: for he hath weighed the world in the balance.
Precept: *Uriel = YOO-rih-el, also known as YOOR-ee-uhl. A prominent Kohathite Levite who helped bring the ark from the home of Obed-edom to Jerusalem; 1 Chronicles 6:24; 15:5, 11*

37 By measure hath he measured the times; and by number hath he numbered the times; and he doth not move nor stir *them*, until the said measure be fulfilled.

38 Then answered I and said, O Lord that bearest rule, even we all are full of impiety.
Precept: *Impiety = Scoffing, Ungodliness, Irreverence towards God, Neglect of the divine precepts, Disobedience to divine commands, Blasphemy*

39 And for our sakes peradventure *it is that* the floors of the righteous are not filled, because of the sins of them that dwell

upon the earth.

40 So he answered me, and said, Go *thy way* to a woman with child, and ask of her when she hath fulfilled her nine months, if her womb may keep the birth any longer within her.

41 Then said I, No, Lord, that can she not. And he said unto me, In the grave the chambers of souls are like the womb *of a woman*:

42 for like as a woman that travaileth maketh haste to escape the necessity of the travail: even so do these *places* haste to deliver those *things* that are committed *unto them*.
Precept: Travail = Agony, Torment, Labor, Task, Effort: Sirach/Ecclesiasticus 19:11 | Genesis 35:16; 38:27 | Exodus 18:8 | Numbers 20:14

43 From the beginning, *look*, what thou desirest to see, it shall be shewed *thee*.

44 Then answered I and said, If I have found favour in thy sight, and if it be possible, and if I be meet *therefore,*

45 shew me *then* whether there be more to come than is past, or more past than is to come.

46 What is past I know, but what is for to come I know not.

47 And he said unto me, Stand *up* upon the right side, and I shall expound the similitude unto thee.
Precept: Similitude(s) = Likeness, Resemblance; Likeness in nature or in appearance: Numbers 12:8 | Deuteronomy 4:12, 15-16 | Psalm 106:20 | Daniel 10:16 | Hosea 12:10

48 So I stood, and saw, and, behold, an hot burning oven passed by before me: and it happened *that* when the flame was gone by I looked, and, behold, the smoke remained still.

49 After this there passed by before me a watery cloud, and sent down much rain with a storm; and when the stormy rain was past, the drops remained still.

50 Then said he unto me, Consider with thyself; as the rain is more than the drops, and as the fire *is greater* than the smoke; but the drops and the smoke remain behind: so the quantity which is past did more exceed.

51 Then I prayed, and said, May I live, thinkest thou, until that time? or what shall happen in those days?

52 He answered me, and said, As for the tokens whereof thou askest me, I may tell thee *of them* in part: but as touching thy life, I am not sent to shew thee; for I do not know *it.*

2 ESDRAS CHAPTER 5

1 Nevertheless as coming the tokens, behold, the days shall come, that *they* which dwell upon earth shall be taken in a great number, and the way of truth shall be hidden, and the land shall be barren of faith.
Precept: Faith = The Spirit of Belief, or the spirit of the believer (Holy Spirit): Galatians 3:6, 24-25 | Jonah 3:5 | Judith 14:10 | John 6:29 | Romans 3:3, 22; 4:3 | James 2:23 | 1 Peter 1:21

2 But iniquity shall be increased above that which *now* thou seest, or that thou hast heard long ago.
Precept: Ezra 9:6 | Jeremiah 30:13-15 | Hosea 4:7 | Matthew 24:12

3 And the land, that thou seest now to have root, shalt thou see wasted *suddenly*.

4 But if the most High grant thee to live, thou shalt see after the third trumpet that the sun shall suddenly shine again in the night, and the moon thrice in the day:
Precept: Revelation 8:10 | Zechariah 14:7

5 and blood shall drop out of wood, and the stone shall give his voice, and the people shall be troubled:
Precept: Luke 19:40

6 and *even* he shall rule, whom they look not for that dwell upon the earth, and the fowls shall take their flight away together:

7 and the Sodomitish sea shall cast out fish, and make a noise in the night, which many have not known: but they shall all hear the voice thereof.
Precept: Sodomitish = Dead, or Dead sea: Joel 2;20 | Ezekiel 47:8

8 There shall be a confusion also in many places, and the fire shall be oft sent out again, and the wild beasts shall change their places, and menstruous women shall bring forth monsters:

9 and salt waters shall be found in the sweet, and all friends shall destroy one another; then shall wit hide itself, and understanding withdraw itself into his secret chamber,

10 and shall be sought of many, and *yet* not be found: then shall unrighteousness and incontinency be multiplied upon earth.
Precept: Incontinency = *Temperance, Self-control* | **Unrighteousness** = *Sin, Wickedness, Injustice, violation of the divine law of God, Ungodly acts, Abomination(s), Fools building upon sand: Matthew 7:26 | Exodus 23:1 | Leviticus 19:15 | Deuteronomy 25:16 | Tobit 4:5; 12:8 | Wisdom 1:5 | Sirach/Ecclesiasticus 7:3; 17:14*

11 *One* land also shall ask another, and say, Is righteousness that maketh *a man* righteous gone through thee? And it shall say, No.

12 At the same time shall men hope, but nothing obtain: they shall labour, but their ways shall not prosper.

13 To shew thee such tokens I have leave; and if thou wilt pray again, and weep as now, and fast even days, thou shalt hear yet greater *things.*

14 Then I awaked, and an extreme fearfulness went through all my body, and my mind was troubled, so that it fainted.
Precept: Psalm 55:5 | Isaiah 21:4 | Deuteronomy 28:66

15 So the angel that was come to talk with me held me, comforted me, and set me *up* upon *my* feet.
Precept: Angel = *appear in a dream is a spirit angel. And angel appear in the flesh is an messenger of the flesh (A Nazarite, vowed to God, many times) of God: Matthew 2:13, 19 in a dream | Genesis 31:11*

16 And in the second night it came to pass, that Salathiel the captain of the people came unto me, saying, Where hast thou been? and why is thy countenance *so* heavy?
Precept: Salathiel = *suh-LAY-thih-el; means: I have asked of Yahawah/God: 1 Chronicles 3:17*

17 Knowest thou not that Israel is committed unto thee in the land of their captivity?

18 Up then, and eat bread, and forsake us not, as the shepherd *that leaveth* his flock in the hands of cruel wolves.

19 Then said I unto him, Go *thy ways* from me, and come not nigh me. And he heard what I said, and went from me.

20 And *so* I fasted seven days, mourning and weeping, like as Uriel the angel commanded me.
Precept: Salathiel = *suh-LAY-th* | *Uriel* = *YOO-rih-el, also known as YOOR-ee-uhl. A prominent Kohathite Levite who helped bring the ark from the home of Obed-edom to Jerusalem; 1 Chronicles 6:24; 15:5, 11* | *Angel* = *appear in a dream is a spirit angel. And angel appear in the flesh is an messenger of the flesh (A Nazarite, vowed to God, many times) of God: Matthew 2:13, 19 in a dream* | *Genesis 31:11*

21 And after seven days so it was, that the thoughts of my heart were very grievous unto me again,
Precept: Grievous = *Oppressive, Onerous, Serious, Powerful curse, burdensome; Causing grief, painful, hard to borne*

22 and my soul recovered the spirit of understanding, and I began to talk with the most High again,

23 and said, O Lord that bearest rule, of every wood of the earth, and *of* all the trees thereof, thou hast chosen *thee* one only vine:

24 and of all lands of the *whole* world thou hast chosen thee one pit: and of all the flowers thereof one lily:

25 and of all the depths of the sea thou hast filled thee one river: and of all builded cities thou hast hallowed Sion unto thyself:

26 and of all the fowls that are created thou hast named thee one dove: and of all the cattle that are made thou hast provided thee

one sheep:
Precept: *Genesis 8:8-11*

27 and among all the multitudes of people thou hast gotten thee one people: and unto this people, whom thou lovedst, thou gavest a law that is approved of all.
Precept: *Deuteronomy 7:8*

28 And now, O Lord, why hast thou given *this* one *people* over unto many? and upon the one root hast thou prepared others, and *why* hast thou scattered thy only one *people* among many?

29 And they which did gainsay thy promises, and believed not thy covenants, have trodden them down.
Precept: Gainsay = *Contradict, Oppose, Deny: Disobedient, to say or speak against*

30 If thou didst so much hate thy people, *yet* shouldest *thou* punish *them* with thine own hands.

31 Now when I had spoken *these* words, the angel that came to me the night afore was sent unto me,
Precept: Angel = *appear in a dream is a spirit angel. And angel appear in the flesh is an messenger of the flesh (A Nazarite, vowed to God, many times) of God: Matthew 2:13, 19 in a dream | Genesis 31:11*

32 And said unto me, Hear me, and I will instruct thee; hearken to the thing that I say, and I shall tell thee more.

33 And I said, Speak *on*, my Lord. Then said he unto me, Thou art sore troubled in mind for Israel's sake: lovest thou that *people* better than *he* that made them?

34 And I said, No, Lord: but of very grief have I spoken: for my reins pain me every hour, while I labour to comprehend the way of the most High, and to seek out part of his judgment.
Precept: Comprehend = *Understand: Job 37:5 | Isaiah 44:18 | Sirach/Ecclesiasticus 32:8*

35 And he said unto me, Thou canst not. And I said, Wherefore, Lord? whereunto was I born *then?* or why was not my mother's womb *then* my grave, that I might not have seen the travail of Jacob, and the wearisome toil of the stock of Israel?
Precept: Travail = *Agony, Torment, Labor, Task, Effort: Sirach/Ecclesiasticus 19:11 | Genesis 35:16; 38:27 | Exodus 18:8 | Numbers 20:14 | Job 3:11*

36 And he said unto me, Number me *the things* that are not yet come, gather me together the drops that are scattered abroad, make me the flowers green again *that are* withered,
Precept: Exodus 5:12 | John 11:52 | Acts 8:1, 4 | Nehemiah 1:8 | Esther 3:8 | 4:11 | Wisdom 11:20 | Matthew 26:31 | James 1:1

37 open me the places that are closed, and bring me forth the winds that in them are shut up, shew me the image of a voice: and then I will declare to thee the thing that thou labourest to know.

38 And I said, O Lord that bearest rule, who may know these *things*, but *he* that hath not his dwelling with men?

39 As for me, I am unwise: how may I then speak of these *things* whereof thou askest me?

40 Then said he unto me, Like as thou canst do none of these *things* that I have spoken of, *even* so canst thou not find out my judgment, or in the end the love that I have promised unto *my* people.

41 And I said, Behold, O Lord, yet art thou nigh unto them that be *reserved* till the end: and what shall they do that have been before me, or *we that be now*, or they that *shall come* after us?

42 And he said unto me, I will liken my judgment unto a ring: like as *there is* no slackness of the last, *even* so *there is* no

swiftness of the first.

43 So I answered and said, Couldest thou not make those that have been made, and be *now*, and that are for to come, at once; that thou mightest shew thy judgment the sooner?

44 Then answered he me, and said, The creature may not haste above the maker; neither *may* the world hold them at once that shall be created therein.

45 And I said, As thou hast said unto thy servant, that thou, which givest life *to all*, hast given life at once to the creature that thou hast created, and the creature bare *it*: *even so* it might now also bear them that *now* be present at once.

46 And he said unto me, Ask the womb of a woman, and say unto her, If thou bringest forth children, why *dost thou it not together*, *but* one after another? pray her therefore to bring forth ten *children* at once.

47 And I said, She cannot: but *must do it* by distance of time.

48 Then said he unto me, Even *so* have I given the womb of the earth to those that be sown in it in *their* times.

49 For like as a young child may not bring forth *the things* that belong to the aged, *even* so have I disposed the world which I created.

50 And I asked, and said, Seeing thou hast now given me the way, I will *proceed to* speak before thee: for our mother, of whom thou hast told me *that* she is young, draweth now nigh unto age.

51 He answered me, and said, Ask a woman that beareth

children, and she shall tell thee.

52 Say unto her, Wherefore are unto *they* whom thou hast now brought forth like those that *were* before, but less of stature?

53 And she shall answer thee, *They* that be born in the strength of youth are of one fashion, and they that are born in the time of age, when the womb faileth, *are* otherwise.

54 Consider thou therefore also, how that ye are less of stature than those that *were* before you.

55 And *so are they* that *come* after you less than ye, as the creatures which now begin to be old, and have passed over the strength of youth.

56 Then said I, Lord, I beseech thee, if I have found favour in thy sight, shew thy servant by whom thou visitest thy creature.

2 ESDRAS CHAPTER 6

1 And he said unto me, In the beginning, when the earth was made, before the borders of the world stood, or ever the winds blew,

2 before it thundered and lightened, or ever the foundations of paradise were laid,

3 before the fair flowers were seen, or ever the moveable powers were established, before the innumerable multitude of angels were gathered together,

Precept: Angel = *appear in a dream is a spirit angel. And angel appear in the flesh is an messenger of the flesh (A Nazarite, vowed to God, many times) of God: Matthew 2:13, 19 in a dream | Genesis 31:11 | Hebrew 12:22*

4 or ever the heights of the air were lifted up, before the measures of the firmament were named, or ever the chimneys in Sion were hot,

Precept: Firmament = *Heaven; Firmament Separated from he earth. The color blue of the sky was attributed to the chaotic waters that the firmament is separated: Genesis 1:7 | Deuteronomy 5:8 | Job 26:11 | 2 Samuel 22:8*

5 and ere the present years were sought out, and or ever the inventions of them that now sin were turned, before they were sealed that have gathered faith for a treasure:

Precept: Faith = *The Spirit of Belief, or the spirit of the believer (Holy Spirit): Galatians 3:6, 24-25 | Jonah 3:5 | Judith 14:10 | John 6:29 | Romans 3:3, 22; 4:3 | James 2:23 | 1 Peter 1:21*

6 then did I consider *these things*, and they *all* were made through me alone, and through none other: by me also they shall be ended, and by none other.

7 Then answered I and said, What *shall be* the parting asunder of the times? or when shall be the end of the first, and the beginning of it that followeth?

8 And he said unto me, From Abraham unto Isaac, when Jacob and Esau were born of him, Jacob's hand held first the heel of Esau.

*Precept: **Esau** = EE-saw; means: Hairy | **Jacob** = JAY-kuhb; means: Supplants | **Abraham** = AY-bruh-ham; means: Father of a multitude: Genesis 25:26*

9 For Esau *is* the end of the world, and Jacob *is* the beginning of it that followeth.

*Precept: **Esau** = EE-saw; means: Hairy | **Jacob** = JAY-kuhb; means: Supplants*

10 The hand of man *is* betwixt the heel and the hand: other *question*, Esdras, ask thou not.

*Precept: **Esdras** = Ez-druhs, is Greek. The Hebrew translation is **Ezra** = Ez-ruh; means: Yahawah is my help*

11 I answered then and said, O Lord that bearest rule, if I have found favour in thy sight,

12 I beseech thee, shew thy servant the end of thy tokens, whereof thou shewedst me part the last night.

13 So he answered and said unto me, Stand up upon thy feet, and hear a mighty sounding voice.

14 And it shall be as it were a *great* motion; but the place where thou standest shall not be moved.

15 And therefore when it speaketh be not afraid: for the word *is* of the end, and the foundation of the earth is understood.

16 And *why?* because the speech of these *things* trembleth and is moved: for it knoweth that the end of these *things* must be changed.

17 And it happened, *that* when I had heard *it* I stood up upon my feet, and hearkened, and, behold, *there was* a voice that spake, and the sound of it *was* like the sound of many waters.

18 And it said, Behold, the days come, that I will begin to draw nigh, and to visit them that dwell upon the earth,

19 and will begin to make inquisition of them, *what they be* that have hurt unjustly with their unrighteousness, and when the affliction of Sion shall be fulfilled;
Precept: Inquisition = Examination, Diligently inquire, Question: Deuteronomy 19:18 | Psalm 9:12 | Esther 2:23 | Unrighteousness = Sin, Wickedness, Injustice, violation of the divine law of God, Ungodly acts, Abomination(s), Fools building upon sand: Matthew 7:26 | Exodus 23:1 | Leviticus 19:15 | Deuteronomy 25:16 | Tobit 4:5; 12:8 | Wisdom 1:5 | Sirach/Ecclesiasticus 7:3; 17:14

20 and when the world, that shall begin to vanish away, shall be finished, *then* will I shew these tokens: the books shall be opened before the firmament, and they shall see all together:
Precept: Firmament = Heaven; Firmament Separated from he earth. The color blue of the sky was attributed to the chaotic waters that the firmament is separated: Genesis 1:7 | Deuteronomy 5:8 | Job 26:11 | 2 Samuel 22:8

21 and the children of a year old shall speak with their voices, the women with child shall bring forth untimely children of three or four months old, and they shall live, and be raised up.

22 And suddenly shall the sown places appear unsown, the full storehouses shall suddenly be found empty:

23 and the trumpet shall give a sound, which when every *man* heareth, they shall be suddenly afraid.

24 At that time shall friends fight one against another like enemies, and the earth shall stand in fear with those *that dwell therein*, the springs of the fountains shall stand still, and in three hours they shall not run.
Precept: Matthew 10:20, 35 | Micah 7:6 | Luke 12:53

25 Whosoever remaineth from all these that I have told thee shall

escape, and see my salvation, and the end of your world.
Precept: Luke 2:30

26 And the men that are received shall see *it*, who have not tasted death from their birth: and the heart of the inhabitants shall be changed, and turned into another meaning.
Precept: Wisdom 18:20 | Matthew 16:28 | John 8:52

27 For evil shall be put out, and deceit shall be quenched.

28 As for faith, it shall flourish, corruption shall be overcome, and the truth, which hath been so long without fruit, shall be declared.
*Precept: **Faith** = The Spirit of Belief, or the spirit of the believer (Holy Spirit): Galatians 3:6, 24-25 | Jonah 3:5 | Judith 14:10 | John 6:29 | Romans 3:3, 22; 4:3 | James 2:23 | 1 Peter 1:21 | **Corruption** = Decay, Decomposition, Sinfulness, Decay life: Isaiah 1:4 | Leviticus 22:24-25 | Psalm 14:1 | Jeremiah 6:28 | Wisdom 14:12, 25 | Sirach/Ecclesiasticus 28:6; 31:5 | **Declared** = Made known, Promised, Manifested: Daniel 4:18 | 2 Esdras 14:35 | 1 Corinthians 3:13 | Declared: Leviticus 23:44 | Deuteronomy 4:13 | Job 26:3 | 1 Esdras 2:24; 3:16 | 2 Esdras 4:4; 6:28 | Tobit 10:8; 13:4 | Judith 8:34; 10:13 |*

29 And when he talked with me, behold, I looked by little and little upon him before whom I stood.

30 And these *words* said he unto me; I am come to shew thee the time of the night to come.

31 If thou wilt pray yet more, and fast seven days again, I shall tell thee greater *things* by day than I have heard.

32 For thy voice is heard before the most High: for the Mighty hath seen *thy* righteous dealing, he hath seen also thy chastity, which thou hast had ever since thy youth.

33 And therefore hath he sent me to shew thee all these *things*, and to say unto thee, Be of good comfort and fear not,
Precept: Joshua 1:9 | Tobit 7:18 | Judith 11:1, 3 | Baruch 4:27 | Matthew 9:22 | Mark 10:49 | Luke 8:48 | 2 Corinthians 13:11 | Philippians 2:19

34 And hasten not with the times that are past, to think vain *things*, that thou mayest not hasten from the latter times.

35 And it came to pass after this, that I wept again, and fasted seven days in like manner, that I might fulfil the three weeks which *he* told me.

36 And in the eighth night was my heart vexed within me again, and I began to speak before the most High.

37 For my spirit was greatly set on fire, and my soul was in distress.

38 And I said, O Lord, thou spakest from the beginning of the creation, even the first day, and saidst thus; Let heaven and earth be made; and thy word *was* a perfect work.
Precept: Heaven = Firmament Separated from he earth. The color blue of the sky was attributed to the chaotic waters that the firmament is separated: Genesis 1:7 | Deuteronomy 5:8 | Job 26:11 | 2 Samuel 22:8 | Genesis 1:1

39 And then was the spirit, and darkness and silence were on every side; the sound of man's voice was not yet formed.
Precept: Genesis 1:2

40 Then commandedst thou a fair light to come forth of thy treasures, that thy work might appear.
Precept: Genesis 1:3 | Psalm 135:7

41 Upon the second day thou madest the spirit of the firmament, and commandedst it to part asunder, and to make a division betwixt the waters, that the one part might go up, and the other remain beneath.
Precept: Firmament = Heaven; Firmament Separated from he earth. The color blue of the sky was attributed to the chaotic waters that the firmament is separated: Genesis 1:6-7 | Deuteronomy 5:8 | Job 26:11 | 2 Samuel 22:8

42 Upon the third day thou didst command that the waters should be gathered in the seventh part of the earth: six parts hast thou dried up, and kept *them*, to the intent that of these *some* being planted of God and tilled might serve thee.
Precept: Genesis 1:9

43 For as soon as thy word went forth the work was made.

44 For immediately there was great and innumerable fruit, and many *and* divers pleasures for the taste, and flowers of unchangeable colour, and odours of wonderful smell: and this was done the third day.
Precept: Genesis 1:11

45 Upon the fourth day thou commandedst that the sun should shine, *and* the moon give her light, *and* the stars should be in order:
Precept: Genesis 1:14

46 and gavest them a charge to do service unto man, that was to be made.
Precept: Genesis 1:15 | Deuteronomy 4:19

47 Upon the fifth day thou saidst unto the seventh part, where the waters were gathered that it should bring forth living creatures, fowls and fishes: and so it came to pass.
Precept: Genesis 1:20, 22

48 *For* the dumb water and without life brought forth living things at the commandment of God, that all people might praise thy wondrous works.
Precept: Genesis 1:20, 22

49 Then didst thou ordain two living creatures, the one thou calledst Enoch, and the other Leviathan;
Precept: Enoch = Personal name meaning: Dedicated | Leviathan = le-vi-ath-un, various meanings: A water monster, Twisting one, Twisted, Coiled: Psalm 74:14; 104:26 | Job 41:1 | Isaiah 27:1

50 and didst separate the one from the other: for the seventh part, (*namely*, where the water was gathered together) might not hold them *both*.

51 Unto Enoch thou gavest one part, which was dried up the third day, that he should dwell in the same part, wherein are a thousand hills:
Precept: Enoch = *Personal name meaning: Dedicated*

52 but unto Leviathan thou gavest the seventh part, *namely*, the moist; and hast kept him to be devoured of whom thou wilt, and when.
Precept: Leviathan = *le-vi-ath-un, various meanings: A water monster, Twisting one, Twisted, Coiled: Psalm 74:14; 104:26 | Job 41:1 | Isaiah 27:1*

53 Upon the sixth day thou gavest commandment unto the earth, that before thee it should bring forth beasts, cattle, and creeping things:
Precept: *Genesis 1:24*

54 and after these, Adam *also*, whom thou madest lord of all thy creatures: of him come we all, and the people also whom thou hast chosen.
Precept: Adam = *Mankind: Genesis 1:26-27*

55 All this have I spoken before thee, O Lord, because thou madest the world for our sakes.

56 As for the other people, which *also* come of Adam, thou hast said that they are nothing, but be like unto spittle: and hast likened the abundance of them unto a drop *that falleth* from a vessel.
Precept: Adam = *Mankind*

57 And now, O Lord, behold, these heathen, which have *ever* been reputed as nothing, have begun to be lords over us, and to

devour us.

58 But we thy people, whom thou hast called *thy* firstborn, *thy* only begotten, and thy fervent lover, are given into their hands.
Precept: Exodus 4:22 | Sirach/Ecclesiasticus 17:18; 36:12

59 If the world now be made for our sakes, why do we not possess an inheritance with the world? how long *shall* this *endure?*

*Precept: **Inheritance** = Passing on of Land, portion of possessions that transfers to an heir upon the owner's physical death: Zechariah 9:2. 1) True inheritance cannot be stolen, brought, or transferred or outside the original owners inherent person: **Revelation** 2:9;3:9 | Numbers 1:18 Transmission from parent to offspring. The acquisition of a possession, condition, or trait from past generations: Amos 3:1-2 | Psalm 147:19-20 2) Something that is inherited by heritage. 3) By birthright of the first born, imperishable heirloom of occupancy: Amos 3:1-2: Psalm 74:10*

2 ESDRAS CHAPTER 7

1 And when I had made an end of speaking these words, there was sent unto me the angel which had been sent unto me the nights afore:

Precept: Angel = appear in a dream is a spirit angel. And angel appear in the flesh is an messenger of the flesh (A Nazarite, vowed to God, many times) of God: Matthew 2:13, 19 in a dream | Genesis 31:11

2 and he said unto me, Up, Esdras, and hear the words that I am come to tell thee.

Precept: Esdras = Ez-druhs, is Greek. The Hebrew translation is Ezra = Ez-ruh; means: Yahawah is my help

3 And I said, Speak *on*, my God. Then said he unto me, The sea is set in a wide place, that it might be deep and great.

Precept: God = Shepherd: Psalm 23:1 | Isaiah 444:28 | Jeremiah 50:6 | Ezekiel 34:23; 37:24

4 But put the case the entrance were narrow, and like a river;

5 Who then could go into the sea to look upon it, and to rule it? if he went not through the narrow, how could he come into the broad?

6 *There is* also another *thing*; A city is builded, and set upon a broad field, and is full of all good *things*:

7 the entrance thereof *is* narrow, and is set in a dangerous place to fall, like as if there were a fire on the right hand, *and* on the left a deep water:

8 and one only path between them *both*, even between the fire and the water, *so small* that there could but one man go there at once.

9 If *this* city now were given unto a man for an inheritance, if he

never shall pass the danger set before *it*, how shall he receive this inheritance?

Precept: Inheritance = *Passing on of Land, portion of possessions that transfers to an heir upon the owner's physical death: Zechariah 9:2. 1) True inheritance cannot be stolen, brought, or transferred or outside the original owners inherent person:* ***Revelation*** *2:9;3:9 | Numbers 1:18 Transmission from parent to offspring. The acquisition of a possession, condition, or trait from past generations: Amos 3:1-2 | Psalm 147:19-20 2) Something that is inherited by heritage. 3) By birthright of the first born, imperishable heirloom of occupancy: Amos 3:1-2*

10 And I said, *It is* so, Lord. Then said he unto me, *Even* so also is Israel's portion.

Precept: Israel = *IZ-ray-el; means: A prince of God*

11 Because for their sakes I made the world: and when Adam transgressed my statutes, *then* was decreed that *now* is done.

Precept: Adam = *Mankind* | *Decreed* = *Ordinance, Resolved, Determined: 2 Chronicles 30:5 | Ezra 6:8 | Romans 13:2 | Numbers 15:15 | Judith 11:13 | Exodus 21:22 | 1 Samuel 20:7*

12 Then were the entrances of this world made narrow, full of sorrow and travail: they *are* but few and evil, full of perils,: and very painful.

Precept: Travail = *Agony, Torment, Labor, Task, Effort: Sirach/Ecclesiasticus 19:11 | Genesis 35:16; 38:27 | Exodus 18:8 | Numbers 20:14 | Perils = Risk of being injured, Destroyed, or Lost, Risk: Lamentations 5:9 | Sirach/Ecclesiasticus 13:13 | 2 Maccabees 1:11 | Romans 8:35 | 2 Timothy 3:1 | Job 5:7; 14:1*

13 For the entrances of the elder world *were* wide and sure, and brought immortal fruit.

Precept: Genesis 2:9 | Sirach/Ecclesiasticus 19:19

14 If then they that live labour not to enter these strait and vain *things*, they can never receive *those* that are laid up *for them*.

Precept: Matthew 7:14 | Strait = Narrow, Tight, Difficult, Strict, Rigorous, Constricted: Exodus 13:19 | Isaiah 49:20 | 1 Samuel 13:6 | Judith 4:7; 14:11

15 Now therefore why disquietest thou thyself, seeing thou art *but* a corruptible *man?* and why art thou moved, whereas thou art *but* mortal?

Precept: Disquietest = *Deprived of quiet, Deprive of peace, or Tranquility*

16 Why hast thou not considered in thy mind *this thing* that is to come, rather than *that* which is present?

17 *Then* answered I and said, O Lord that bearest rule, thou hast ordained in thy law, that the righteous should inherit these *things*, but *that* the ungodly should perish.

*Precept: **Inherit** = Inheritance = Passing on of Land, portion of possessions that transfers to an heir upon the owner's physical death: Zechariah 9:2. 1) True inheritance cannot be stolen, brought, or transferred or outside the original owners inherent person: Revelation 2:9;3:9 | Numbers 1:18 Transmission from parent to offspring. The acquisition of a possession, condition, or trait from past generations: Amos 3:1-2 | Psalm 147:19-20 2) Something that is inherited by heritage. 3) By birthright of the first born, imperishable heirloom of occupancy: Amos 3:1-2 | Deuteronomy 8:1*

18 Nevertheless the righteous shall suffer strait *things*, and hope for wide: for they that have done wickedly have suffered the strait *things*, and yet shall not see the wide.

*Precept: **Strait** = Narrow, Tight, Difficult, Strict, Rigorous, Constricted: Exodus 13:19 | Isaiah 49:20 | 1 Samuel 13:6 | Judith 4:7; 14:11*

19 And he said unto me. There is no judge above God, and none that hath understanding above the Highest.

20 For *there be* many *that* perish in this life, because they despise the law of God that is set before *them*.

21 For God hath given strait commandment to such as came, what they should do to live, *even* as they came, and what they should observe to avoid punishment.

*Precept: **Strait** = Narrow, Tight, Difficult, Strict, Rigorous, Constricted: Exodus 13:19 | Isaiah 49:20 | 1 Samuel 13:6 | Judith 4:7; 14:11*

22 Nevertheless they were not obedient *unto him*; but spake against him, and imagined vain things;

23 and deceived themselves by their wicked deeds; and said *of* the most High, that *he* is not; and knew not his ways:

Precept: Deceived = *Beguiled, Fooled, in Error, Taught to sin: 2 Samuel 6:7 | Isaiah 32:6 | 1 Esdras 9:20 | Tobit 5:13 | Judith 5:20 | Wisdom 1:12 | Sirach/Ecclesiasticus 11:16 | Genesis 3:13 | Numbers 25:18 | Esther 16:6 | Wisdom 4:11*

24 but his law have they despised, and denied his covenants; in his statutes have they not been faithful, and have not performed his works.

Precept: Faith = *The Spirit of Belief, or the spirit of the believer (Holy Spirit): Galatians 3:6, 24-25 | Jonah 3:5 | Judith 14:10 | John 6:29 | Romans 3:3, 22; 4:3 | James 2:23 | 1 Peter 1:21 | Faithful = Trustful, trustworthy*

25 *And* therefore, Esdras, for the empty *are* empty *things*, and for the full *are* the full *things*.

Precept: Esdras = *Ez-druhs, is Greek. The Hebrew translation is Ezra = Ez-ruh; means: Yahawah is my help*

26 Behold, the time shall come, that *these* tokens which I have told thee shall come to pass, and the bride shall appear, and she coming forth shall be seen, that now is withdrawn from the earth.

27 And whosoever is delivered from the foresaid evils shall see my wonders.

28 For my son Jesus shall be revealed with those that be with him, and they that remain shall rejoice within four hundred years.

Precept: Daniel 9:26-27 | Jesus or Yahawashi = YAH-how-WAH-shi: Deuteronomy 18:15, 18-19 | Isaiah 40:5; 56:1 | John 1:45 | Acts 7:37

29 After these years shall my son Christ die, and all men that have life.

Precept: Daniel 9:26-27

30 And the world shall be turned into the old silence seven days, like as in the former judgments: so that no man shall remain.

31 And after seven days the world, that yet awaketh not, shall be raised up, and that shall die that is corrupt

32 And the earth shall restore *those* that are asleep in her, and *so* shall the dust *those* that dwell in silence, and the secret places shall deliver *those* souls that were committed unto them.
Precept: Isaiah 26:19 | Daniel 12:2

33 And the most High shall appear upon the seat of judgment, and misery shall pass away, and the long suffering shall have an end:
Precept: Matthew 25:31

34 but judgment only shall remain, truth shall stand, and faith shall wax strong:
Precept: Faith = The Spirit of Belief, or the spirit of the believer (Holy Spirit): Galatians 3:6, 24-25 | Jonah 3:5 | Judith 14:10 | John 6:29 | Romans 3:3, 22; 4:3 | James 2:23 | 1 Peter 1:21

35 and the work shall follow, and the reward shall be shewed, and the good deeds shall be of force, and wicked deeds shall bear no rule.
Precept: Revelation 14:13 | Matthew 16:27 | Psalm 62:12

36 Then said I, Abraham prayed first for the Sodomites, and Moses for the fathers that sinned in the wilderness:
Precept: Abraham = AY-bruh-ham; means: Father of a multitude: Genesis 18:23 | Exodus 32:11

37 And Jesus after him for Israel in the time of Achan:
Precept: Israel = IZ-ray-el; means: A prince of God

38 and Samuel *and* David for the destruction: and Solomon for them that should come to the sanctuary:
Precept: Solomon = SAHL-uh-muhn; means: Will give Shalom, The LORD's beloved | David = DAY-vid. The name David is a suggested title to the throne, not a personal name; means: The True Messiah

39 and Helias for those that received rain; and for the dead, that he might live:
Precept: Helias = HEE-lee-uhs

40 and Ezechias for the people in the time of Sennacherib: and many for many.
*Precept: Ezechias = ez-uh-KIGH-uhs. The Hebrew translation is **Jahzeiah** = jay-huh-ZIGH-uh; means: Yahawah sees, reveals:Ezra 10:15 | **Sennacherib** = such-nAK-uh-rib*

41 Even so now, seeing corruption is grown up, and wickedness increased, and the righteous have prayed for the ungodly: wherefore shall it not be so now also?
Precept: Corruption = Decay, Decomposition, Sinfulness, Decay life: Isaiah 1:4 | Leviticus 22:24-25 | Psalm 14:1 | Jeremiah 6:28 | Wisdom 14:12, 25 | Sirach/ Ecclesiasticus 28:6; 31:5

42 He answered me, and said, *This* present life is not the end where much glory doth abide; therefore have they prayed for the weak.

43 But the day of doom shall be the end of this time, and the beginning of the immortality for to come, wherein corruption is past,
Precept: Corruption = Decay, Decomposition, Sinfulness, Decay life: Isaiah 1:4 | Leviticus 22:24-25 | Psalm 14:1 | Jeremiah 6:28 | Wisdom 14:12, 25 | Sirach/ Ecclesiasticus 28:6; 31:5 | 1 Corinthians 15:54

44 intemperance is at an end, infidelity is cut off, righteousness is grown, *and* truth is sprung up.
Precept: Intemperance = IN-tem-per-ance: Drunkenness, Drunk, Excessive drinking of intoxicants

45 Then shall no man be able to save him that is destroyed, nor to oppress *him* that hath gotten the victory.
Precept: Psalm 49:7-8 | Deuteronomy 28:29, 68

46 I answered then and said, This is my first and last saying, that it had been better not to have given the earth unto Adam: or else, when it was given *him*, to have restrained him from sinning.

47 For what profit is it for men *now* in this present time to live in heaviness, and after death to look for punishment?

Precept: Ecclesiastes 2:22-23

48 O thou Adam, what hast thou done? for though it was thou that sinned, thou art not fallen alone, but we *all* that come of thee.

49 For what profit is it unto us, if there be promised us an immortal time, whereas we have done the works that bring death?

50 And that there is promised us an everlasting hope, whereas ourselves being most wicked are made vain?

51 And that there are laid up for us dwellings of health and safety, whereas we have lived wickedly?

52 And that the glory of the most High is kept to defend them which have led a wary life, whereas we have walked in the most wicked ways *of all?*

53 And that there should be shewed a paradise, whose fruit endureth for ever, wherein is security and medicine, since we shall not enter *into it?*

54 (For we have walked in unpleasant places.)

55 And that the faces of them which have used abstinence shall shine above the stars, whereas our faces *shall be* blacker than darkness?
Precept: Abstinence = Temperance

56 For while we lived and committed iniquity, we considered not that we should begin to suffer *for it* after death.

57 Then answered he *me*, and said, This is the condition of the battle, which man that is born upon the earth shall fight;

58 That, if he be overcome, he shall suffer as thou hast said: but if he get the victory, he shall receive *the thing* that I say.

59 For this is the life whereof Moses spake unto the people while he lived, saying, Choose thee life, that thou mayest live.
Precept: *Deuteronomy 30:19*

60 Nevertheless they believed not him, nor yet the prophets after him, no nor me which have spoken unto them,

61 that there should not be *such* heaviness in their destruction, as shall be joy over them that are persuaded to salvation.

62 I answered then, and said, I know, Lord, that the most High is called merciful, in that he hath mercy upon them which are not yet come into the world,

63 And upon those *also* that turn to his law;

64 And *that* he is patient, and long suffereth those that have sinned, as his creatures;

65 And *that* he is bountiful, for he is ready to give where it needeth;

66 And *that he is* of great mercy, for he multiplieth more *and more* mercies to them that are present, and that are past, and *also to them* which are to come.

67 For if he shall not multiply his mercies, the world would not continue with them that inherit therein.

68 And he pardoneth; for if he did not so of his goodness, that they which have committed iniquities might be eased of them,

the ten thousandth part of men should not remain living.

69 And being judge, if he should not forgive them that are cured with his word, and put out the multitude of contentions,
Precept: **Contentions** = *Strife, Struggles*

70 There should be very few left peradventure in an innumerable multitude.
Precept: **Peradventure** = *PEAR-uh-vent-ture; Haply; Perhaps, possibly, Maybe: Genesis 18:24; 42:4 | Exodus 32:30 | Joshua 9:7*

2 ESDRAS CHAPTER 8

1 And he answered me, saying, The most High hath made this world for many, but the world to come for few.

2 I will tell thee a similitude, Esdras; As when thou askest the earth, it shall say unto thee, that it giveth much mould whereof earthen vessels are made, but little dust that gold cometh of: even so is the course of *this* present world.
Precept: **Esdras** = *Ez-druhs, is Greek. The Hebrew translation is* **Ezra** = *Ez-ruh; means: Yahawah is my help* | **Similitude(s)** = *Likeness, Resemblance; Likeness in nature or in appearance: Numbers 12:8 | Deuteronomy 4:12, 15-16 | Psalm 106:20 | Daniel 10:16 | Hosea 12:10*

3 There be many created, but few shall be saved.
Precept: Matthew 20;16; 22;1

4 So answered I and said, Swallow then down, O *my* soul, understanding, and devour wisdom.

5 For thou hast agreed to give ear, and *art* willing to prophesy: for thou hast no longer space than only to live.

6 O Lord, if thou suffer not thy servant, that we may pray before thee, and thou give us seed unto our heart, and culture to *our* understanding, that there may come fruit of it; how shall each *man* live that is corrupt, who beareth the place of a man?

7 For thou art alone, and we *all* one workmanship of thine hands, like as thou hast said.
Precept: Isaiah 64:8

8 For when the body is fashioned now in the *mother's* womb, and thou givest *it* members, thy creature is preserved in fire and water, and nine months doth thy workmanship endure thy creature which is created in her.

9 But that which keepeth and is kept shall both be preserved: and when the time cometh, the womb preserved delivereth up *the things* that grew in it.

10 For thou hast commanded out of the parts of the body, that is to say, *out of* the breasts, milk to be given, which is the fruit of the breasts,

11 that the thing which is fashioned may be nourished for a time, till thou disposest it to thy mercy.

12 Thou broughtest it up with thy righteousness, and nurturedst it in thy law, and reformedst it with thy judgment.

13 And thou shalt mortify it as thy creature, and quicken it as thy work.
Precept: Mortify = To subdue or deaden (as the body or bodily appetites)

14 If therefore thou shalt destroy him which with so great labour was fashioned, it is an easy *thing* to be ordained by thy commandment, that the thing which was made might be preserved.

15 Now therefore, Lord, I will speak; touching man in general, thou knowest best; but touching thy people, for whose sake I am sorry;

16 and for thine inheritance, for whose cause I mourn; and for Israel, for whom I am heavy; and for Jacob, for whose sake I am troubled;
Precept: Israel = IZ-ray-el; means: A prince of God | Jacob = JAY-kuhb; means: Supplants | Inheritance = Passing on of Land, portion of possessions that transfers to an heir upon the owner's physical death: Zechariah 9:2. 1) True inheritance cannot be stolen, brought, or transferred or outside the original owners inherent person: Revelation 2:9;3:9 | Numbers 1:18 Transmission from parent to offspring. The acquisition of a possession, condition, or trait from past generations: Amos 3:1-2 | Psalm 147:19-20 2) Something that is inherited by heritage. 3) By birthright of the first born, imperishable heirloom of occupancy: Amos 3:1-2

17 therefore will I begin to pray before thee for myself and for them: for I see the falls of us that dwell in the land.

18 But I have heard the swiftness of the judge which is to come.

19 Therefore hear my voice, and understand my words, and I shall speak before thee. *This is* the beginning of the words of Esdras, before he was taken up: and I said,
Precept: Esdras = *Ez-druhs, is Greek. The Hebrew translation is* ***Ezra*** = *Ez-ruh; means: Yahawah is my help*

20 O Lord, thou that dwellest in everlastingness which beholdest from above *things* in the heaven and in the air;
Precept: Heaven = *Firmament Separated from he earth. The color blue of the sky was attributed to the chaotic waters that the firmament is separated: Genesis 1:7 | Deuteronomy 5:8 | Job 26:11 | 2 Samuel 22:8*

21 whose throne is inestimable; whose glory may not be comprehended; before whom the hosts of angels stand with trembling,
Precept: Angel = *appear in a dream is a spirit angel. And angel appear in the flesh is an messenger of the flesh (A Nazarite, vowed to God, many times) of God: Matthew 2:13, 19 in a dream | Genesis 31:11 |* ***Inestimable*** = *in-es-ti-ma-ble; Incapable of being estimated or computed |* ***Comprehend*** = *Understand: Job 37:5 | Isaiah 44:18 | Sirach/Ecclesiasticus 32:8*

22 (whose service is conversant in wind and fire,) whose word *is* true, and sayings constant; whose commandment *is* strong, and ordinance fearful;

23 whose look drieth up the depths, and indignation maketh the mountains to melt away; which the truth witnesseth:
Precept: Indignation = *IN-dig-nation: Anger aroused, Dissatisfaction, Disfavor, Dislike, Unjust, Unworthy, Extreme anger, Disgust: 2 Kings 3:27 | Nehemiah 4:1 | Esther 5:9 | Job 10:17 | Psalms 69:24; 102;10 | Micah 7:9 | Habakkuk 3:12 | Sirach/Ecclesiasticus 5:6; 36:7 | Baruch 2:20 | Bel 28*

24 O hear the prayer of thy servant, and give ear to the petition of

thy creature.

25 For while I live I will speak, and so long as I have understanding I will answer.

26 O look not upon the sins of thy people; but *on them* which serve thee in truth.

27 Regard not the wicked inventions of the heathen, but *the desire of those* that keep thy testimonies in afflictions.

28 Think not *upon those* that have walked feignedly before thee: but remember *them*, which according to thy will have known *thy* fear.
Precept: Feignedly/Feigned = Ridiculously, Pretend: Jeremiah 3:10 | 1 Samuel 21:13 | 2 Samuel 14:2 | Psalm 17:1

29 Let it not be thy will to destroy *them* which have lived like beasts; but to look upon them that have clearly taught thy law.

30 Take thou no indignation at them which are deemed worse than beasts; but love them that always put their trust in thy righteousness and glory.
Precept: Indignation = IN-dig-nation: Anger aroused, Dissatisfaction, Disfavor, Dislike, Unjust, Unworthy, Extreme anger, Disgust: 2 Kings 3:27 | Nehemiah 4:1 | Esther 5:9 | Job 10:17 | Psalms 69:24; 102:10 | Micah 7:9 | Habakkuk 3:12 | Sirach/ Ecclesiasticus 5:6; 36:7 | Baruch 2:20 | Bel 28

31 For we and our fathers do languish of such diseases: but because of us sinners thou shalt be called merciful.
Precept: Languish = Feeble, Weak, Spiritless: Isaiah 16:8; 19:8 | Jeremiah 14:2 | Hosea 4:3

32 For if thou hast a desire to have mercy upon us, thou shalt be called merciful, to us namely, that have no works of righteousness.

33 For the just, which have many *good* works laid up *with thee,* shall out of their own deeds receive reward.

34 For what is man, that thou shouldest take displeasure at him? or *what is* a corruptible generation, that thou shouldest be so bitter toward it?

35 For in truth them is no man among them that be born, but he hath dealt wickedly; and among the faithful *there is none* which hath not done amiss.
Precept: Faith = *The Spirit of Belief, or the spirit of the believer (Holy Spirit): Galatians 3:6, 24-25 | Jonah 3:5 | Judith 14:10 | John 6:29 | Romans 3:3, 22; 4:3 | James 2:23 | 1 Peter 1:21*

36 For in this, O Lord, thy righteousness and thy goodness shall be declared, if thou be merciful unto them which have not the confidence of good works.
Precept: Declared = *Made known, Promised, Manifested: Daniel 4:18 | 2 Esdras 14:35 | 1 Corinthians 3:13 | Declared: Leviticus 23:44 | Deuteronomy 4:13 | Job 26:3 | 1 Esdras 2:24; 3:16 | 2 Esdras 4:4; 6:28 | Tobit 10:8; 13:4 | Judith 8:34; 10:13 |*

37 Then answered he me, and said, Some *things* hast thou spoken aright, and according unto thy words it shall be.

38 For indeed I will not think on the disposition of them which have sinned before death, before judgment, before destruction:
Precept: Disposition = *Administration, Control, Settlement, temperament, Character, Personality: Sirach/Ecclesiasticus 20:26 | Judith 8:29 | Rest of Esther 16:6*

39 but I will rejoice over the disposition of the righteous, and I will remember also *their* pilgrimage, and the salvation, and the reward, that they shall have.
Precept: Disposition = *Administration, Control, Settlement, temperament, Character, Personality: Sirach/Ecclesiasticus 20:26 | Judith 8:29 | Rest of Esther 16:6*

40 Like as I have spoken now, so shall it come to pass.

41 For as the husbandman soweth much seed upon the ground,

and planteth many trees, and yet *the thing* that is sown *good* in his season cometh not up, neither doth all that is planted take root: even so *is it of them* that are sown in the world; they shall not all be saved.

42 I answered then and said, If I have found grace, let me speak.

43 Like as the husbandman's seed *perisheth*, if it come not up, and receive not thy rain in due season; or if there come too much rain, and corrupt it:

44 Even so perisheth man also, which is formed with thy hands, and is called thine own image, because thou art like unto him, for whose sake thou hast made all *things*, and likened him unto the husbandman's seed.

45 Be not wroth with us but spare thy people, and have mercy upon thine own inheritance: for thou art merciful unto thy creature.

*Precept: **Inheritance** = Passing on of Land, portion of possessions that transfers to an heir upon the owner's physical death: Zechariah 9:2. 1) True inheritance cannot be stolen, brought, or transferred or outside the original owners inherent person: **Revelation** 2:9;3:9 | Numbers 1:18 Transmission from parent to offspring. The acquisition of a possession, condition, or trait from past generations: Amos 3:1-2 | Psalm 147:19-20. 2) Something that is inherited by heritage. 3) By birthright of the first born, imperishable heirloom of occupancy: Amos 3:1-2 | Joel 2;17*

46 Then answered he me, and said, *Things* present *are* for the present, and *things* to cometh for such as be to come.

47 For thou comest far short that thou shouldest be able to love my creature more than I: but I have ofttimes drawn nigh unto thee, and unto it, but never to the unrighteous.

48 In this also thou art marvellous before the most High:

49 in that thou hast humbled thyself, as it becometh thee, and

132

hast not judged thyself *worthy* to be much glorified among the righteous.

50 For many great miseries shall be done to them that in the latter *time* shall dwell in the world, because they have walked in great pride.

51 But understand thou for thyself, and seek out the glory for such as be like thee.

52 For unto you is paradise opened, the tree of life is planted, the time to come is prepared, plenteousness is made ready, a city is builded, and rest is allowed, yea, perfect goodness and wisdom.
Precept: Revelation 22:2; 21:2

53 The root of evil is sealed up from you, weakness and the moth is hid from you, and corruption is fled into hell to be forgotten:
Precept: Corruption = *Decay, Decomposition, Sinfulness, Decay life: Isaiah 1:4 | Leviticus 22:24-25 | Psalm 14:1 | Jeremiah 6:28 | Wisdom 14:12, 25 | Sirach/ Ecclesiasticus 28:6; 31:5 | Psalm 39:11*

54 sorrows are passed, and in the end is shewed the treasure of immortality.

55 *And* therefore ask thou no more questions concerning the multitude of them that perish.

56 For when they had taken liberty, they despised the most High, thought scorn of his law, and forsook his ways.

57 Moreover they have trodden down his righteous,

58 and said in their heart, that there is no God; yea, and that knowing they must die.
Precept: Psalm 14:1; 53:1 | Isaiah 44:6

59 For as the *things* aforesaid shalt receive you, so thirst and pain

are prepared for them: for it was not his will that men should come to nought:

60 but they which be created have defiled the name of him that made them, and were unthankful unto him which prepared life for them.

61 And therefore is my judgment now at hand.

62 These *things* have I not shewed unto all *men*, but unto thee, and a few like thee. Then answered I and said,

63 Behold, O Lord, now hast thou shewed me the multitude of the wonders, which thou wilt begin to do in the last *times*: but at what time, thou hast not shewed me.

2 ESDRAS CHAPTER 9

1 He answered me then, and said, Measure thou the time diligently in itself: and when thou seest part of the signs past, which I have told *thee* before,

Precept: Diligently = Diligence: Of high value, upmost importance: Deuteronomy 4:9; 6:17 | Psalms 77:6; 119:4 | 2 Esdras 9:1; 13:54 | Wisdom 7:13; 13:7 | Sirach/ Ecclesiasticus 18:14; 27:3 | Susanna 12 | Proverbs 10:4

2 then shalt thou understand, that it is the very *same* time, wherein the Highest will begin to visit the world which he made.

3 Therefore when there shall be seen earthquakes and uproars of the people in the world:

4 Then shalt thou *well* understand, that the most High spake of those *things* from the days that were before thee, *even* from the beginning.

5 For like as all that is made in the world hath a beginning and an end, and the end is manifest:

6 *even* so the times also of the Highest have plain beginnings in wonder and powerful works, and endings in effects and signs.

7 And every one that shall be saved, and shall be able to escape by his works, and by faith, whereby ye have believed,

Precept: Faith = The Spirit of Belief, or the spirit of the believer (Holy Spirit): Galatians 3:6, 24-25 | Jonah 3:5 | Judith 14:10 | John 6:29 | Romans 3:3, 22; 4:3 | James 2:23 | 1 Peter 1:21

8 shall be preserved from the said perils, and shall see my salvation in my land, and within my borders: for I have sanctified *them for* me from the beginning.

Precept: Perils = Risk of being injured, Destroyed, or Lost, Risk: Lamentations 5:9 | Sirach/Ecclesiasticus 13:13 | 2 Maccabees 1:11 | Romans 8:35 | 2 Timothy 3:1

9 Then shall they be in pitiful case, which now have abused my ways: and they that have cast them away despitefully shall dwell in torments.

10 For such as in their life have received benefits, and have not known me;

11 and *they* that have loathed my law, while they had yet liberty, and, when as yet place of repentance was open unto them, understood not, but despised *it*;

12 the same must know *it* after death by pain.

13 And therefore be thou not curious how the ungodly shall be punished, and when: but enquire how the righteous shall be saved, whose the world is, and for whom the world *is created*.

14 Then answered I and said,

15 I have said before, and now do speak, and will speak *it also* hereafter, that there be *many* more *of them* which perish, than *of them* which shall be saved:

16 like as a wave is greater than a drop.

17 And he answered me, saying, Like as the field *is*, so *is* also the seed; as the flowers *be*, such *are* the colours also; such as the workman *is*, such also *is* the work; and as the husbandman *is himself*, so *is his* husbandry *also*: for it was the time of the world.
Precept: Husbandry = Land, Ground, the Land/Ground, (love the land/ground, or cursed): Genesis 2:9; 3:17; 9:20

18 And now when I prepared the world, which was not yet made, even for them to dwell in that now live, no man spake against me.

19 For then every one *obeyed*: but now the manners of them which are created in this world that is made are corrupted by a perpetual seed, and by a law which is unsearchable rid themselves.

20 So I considered the world, and, behold, there was peril because of the devices that were come into it.
Precept: *Malachi 3:17*

21 And I saw, and spared it greatly, and have kept me a grape of the cluster, and a plant of a great people.

22 Let the multitude perish then, which was born in vain; and let my grape be kept, and my plant; for with great labour have I made *it* perfect.

23 Nevertheless, if thou wilt cease yet seven days more, (but thou shalt not fast in them,

24 *but* go into a field of flowers, where no house is builded, and eat only the flowers of the field; taste no flesh, drink no wine, but *eat* flowers only;)

25 *and* pray unto the Highest continually, then will I come and talk with thee.

26 So I went my way into the field which is called Ardath, like as he commanded me; and there I sat among the flowers, and did eat of the herbs of the field, and the meat of the same satisfied me.
Precept: Ardath *= AHR-dath; A field Ezra communed with Yahawah*

27 After seven days I sat upon the grass, and my heart was vexed *within me*, like as before:

28 And I opened my mouth, and began to talk before the most

High, and said,

29 O Lord, thou that shewest thyself unto us, thou wast shewed unto our fathers in the wilderness, *in a place* where no man treadeth, in a barren *place*, when they came out of Egypt.

30 And thou spakest saying, Hear me, O Israel; and mark my words, *thou* seed of Jacob.
Precept: **Israel** = *IZ-ray-el; means: A prince of God* | **Jacob** = *JAY-kuhb; means: Supplants*

31 For, behold, I sow my law in you, and it shall bring fruit in you, and ye shall be honoured in it for ever.

32 But our fathers, which received the law, kept *it* not, and observed not thy ordinances: and though the fruit of *thy* law did not perish, neither could it, for it was thine;
Precept: **Ordinances** = *Order, specific directions, seen as Law of direction: Exodus 18:20 | Leviticus 18:3, 30*

33 yet *they* that received *it* perished, because they kept not *the thing* that was sown in them.

34 And, lo, it is a custom, when the ground hath received seed, or the sea a ship, or any vessel meat or drink, that, that being perished wherein it was sown or cast into,

35 that *thing* also which was sown, or cast therein, or received, doth perish, and remaineth not with us: but with us it hath not happened so.

36 For we that have received the law perish by sin, and our heart *also* which received it

37 Notwithstanding the law perisheth not, but remaineth in his force.

38 And when I spake these *things* in my heart, I looked back with mine eyes, and upon the right side I saw a woman, and, behold, she mourned and wept with a loud voice, and was much grieved in heart, and her clothes *were* rent, and *she had* ashes upon her head.

39 Then let I my thoughts go that I was in, and turned me unto her,

40 and said unto her, Wherefore weepest thou? why art thou so grieved in *thy* mind?

41 And she said unto me, Sir, let me alone, that I may bewail myself, and add unto my sorrow, for I am sore vexed in my mind, and brought very low.

42 And I said unto her, What aileth thee? tell me.

43 She said unto me, I thy servant have been barren, and had no child, though I had an husband thirty years,

44 and those thirty years I did nothing else day and night, and every hour, but make my, prayer to the Highest.

45 After thirty years God heard me thine handmaid, looked upon my misery, considered my trouble, and gave me a son: and I was very glad of him, *so was* my husband also, and all my neighbours: and we gave great honour unto the Almighty.
*Precept: **Neighbour(s)*** *= One who is a fellow Israelite, Members of a community united by divine covenant, law, and teachings, the Israelites' obligations to Yahawah (God): Exodus 2:13; 19:6; 22:25-26 | Leviticus 19:13, 15-17 | Deuteronomy 15:7-11 | 1 Samuel 28:17*

46 And I nourished him with great travail.
*Precept: **Travail*** *= Agony, Torment, Labor, Task, Effort: Sirach/Ecclesiasticus 19:11 | Genesis 35:16; 38:27 | Exodus 18:8 | Numbers 20:14*

47 So when he grew up, and came to the time that he should have a wife, I made a feast.

2 ESDRAS CHAPTER 10

1 And it so came to pass, *that* when my son was entered into his wedding chamber, he fell down, and died.

2 Then we all overthrew the lights, and all my neighbours rose up to comfort me: so I took my rest unto the second day at night.
Precept: Neighbour(s) *= One who is a fellow Israelite, Members of a community united by divine covenant, law, and teachings, the Israelites' obligations to Yahawah (God): Exodus 2:13; 19:6; 22:25-26 | Leviticus 19:13, 15-17 | Deuteronomy 15:7-11 | 1 Samuel 28:17*

3 And it came to pass, when they had all left off to comfort me, to the end I might be quiet; then rose I up by night and fled, and came *hither* into this field, as thou seest.

4 And I do now purpose not to return into the city, but here to stay, and neither to eat nor drink, but continually to mourn and to fast until I die.

5 Then left I the meditations wherein I was, and spake to her in anger, saying,

6 *Thou* foolish woman above all other, seest thou not our mourning, and what happeneth unto us?

7 How that Sion our mother is full of all heaviness, and much humbled, mourning very sore?

8 And now, seeing we all mourn and are sad, for we are all in heaviness, art thou grieved for one son?

9 For ask the earth, and she shall tell thee, that it is she which ought to mourn for the fall of so many that grow upon her.

10 For out of her came all at the first, and *out of her* shall *all*

others come, and, behold, they walk almost all into destruction, and a multitude of them is utterly rooted out.

11 Who then should make more mourning than she, that hath lost so great a multitude; and not thou, which art sorry but for one?

12 But if thou sayest unto me, My lamentation is not like the earth's, because I have lost the fruit of my womb, which I brought forth with pains, and bare with sorrows;

13 but the earth *not so*: for the multitude present in it according to the course of the earth is gone, as it came:

14 then say I unto thee, Like as thou hast brought forth with labour; *even* so the earth also hath given her fruit, *namely*, man, ever since the beginning unto him that made her.

15 Now therefore keep thy sorrow to thyself, and bear with a good courage that which hath befallen thee.

16 For if thou shalt acknowledge the determination of God to be just, thou shalt both receive thy son in time, and shalt be commended among women.

17 Go thy way then into the city to thine husband.

18 And she said unto me, *That* will I not do: I will not go into the city, but here will I die.

19 So I proceeded to speak further unto her, and said,

20 Do not so, but be counselled. by me: for how many *are* the adversities of Sion? be comforted in regard of the sorrow of Jerusalem.

21 For thou seest that our sanctuary is laid waste, our altar broken down, our temple destroyed;

22 our psaltery is laid on the ground, *our* song is put to silence, our rejoicing is at an end, the light of our candlestick is put out, the ark of our covenant is spoiled, our holy *things* are defiled, and the name that is called upon us is almost profaned: our children are put to shame, our priests are burnt, our Levites are gone into captivity, our virgins are defiled, and our wives ravished; our righteous *men* carried away, our little ones destroyed, our young men are brought in bondage, and our strong *men* are become weak;

Precept: Priests = *Called Ministers*

23 and, which *is* the greatest of all, the seal of Sion hath now lost her honour; for she is delivered into the hands of them that hate us.

24 And therefore shake off thy great heaviness, and put away the multitude of sorrows, that the Mighty may be merciful unto thee again, and the Highest shall give thee rest *and* ease from thy labour.

25 And it came to pass while I was talking with her, *behold*, her face upon a sudden shined exceedingly, and her countenance glistered, so that I was afraid of her, and mused what it might be.

26 And, behold, suddenly she made a great cry very fearful: so that the earth shook at the noise of the woman.

27 And I looked, and, behold, the woman appeared unto me no more, but there was a city builded, and a large place shewed itself from the foundations: then was I afraid, and cried with a loud voice, and said,

28 Where is Uriel the angel, who came unto me at the first? for

he hath caused me to fall into many trances, and mine end is turned into corruption, and my prayer to rebuke.

Precept: Uriel = YOO-rih-el, also known as YOOR-ee-uhl. A prominent Kohathite Levite who helped bring the ark from the home of Obed-edom to Jerusalem; 1 Chronicles 6:24; 15:5, 11 | Angel = appear in a dream is a spirit angel. And angel appear in the flesh is an messenger of the flesh (A Nazarite, vowed to God, many times) of God: Matthew 2:13, 19 in a dream | Genesis 31:11 | Corruption = Decay, Decomposition, Sinfulness, Decay life: Isaiah 1:4 | Leviticus 22:24-25 | Psalm 14:1 | Jeremiah 6:28 | Wisdom 14:12, 25 | Sirach/Ecclesiasticus 28:6; 31:5

29 And as I was speaking these *words* behold, he came unto me, and looked upon me.

30 And, lo, I lay as one that had been dead, and mine understanding was taken *from me*: and he took me by the right hand, and comforted me, and set me upon my feet, and said unto me,

31 What aileth thee? and why art thou *so* disquieted? and why is thine understanding troubled, and the thoughts of thine heart?

32 And I said, Because thou hast forsaken me, and yet I did according to thy words, and I went into the field, and, lo, I have seen, and *yet* see, that I am not able to express.

33 And he said unto me, Stand *up* manfully, and I will advise thee.

34 Then said I, Speak *on*, my lord, in me; *only* forsake me not, lest I die frustrate *of my hope*.

35 For I have seen that I knew not, and hear that I do not know.

36 Or is my sense deceived, or my soul in a dream?

37 Now therefore I beseech thee that thou wilt shew thy servant of this vision.

38 He answered me then, and said, Hear me, and I shall inform thee, and tell thee wherefore thou art afraid: for the Highest will reveal many secret things unto thee.

39 He hath seen that thy way is right: for that thou sorrowest continually for thy people, and makest great lamentation for Sion.

40 This therefore is the meaning of the vision which thou lately sawest:

41 thou sawest a woman mourning, and thou begannest to comfort her:

42 But now seest thou the likeness of the woman no more, but there appeared unto thee a city builded.

43 And whereas she told thee of the death of her son, this is the solution:

44 this woman, whom thou sawest is Sion: and whereas she said unto thee, even she whom thou seest as a city builded,

45 Whereas, I *say*, she said unto thee, that she hath been thirty years barren: those are the thirty years wherein there was no offering made in her.

46 But after thirty years Solomon builded the city and offered offerings: and then bare the barren a son.
Precept: Solomon = *SAHL-uh-muhn; means: Will give Shalom, The LORD's beloved*

47 And whereas she told thee that she nourished him with labour: that was the dwelling in Jerusalem.

48 But whereas she said unto thee, That my son coming into his marriage chamber happened to have a fail, and died: this was the destruction that came to Jerusalem.

49 And, behold, thou sawest her likeness, and because she mourned for her son, thou begannest to comfort her: and of these *things* which have chanced, these are to be opened unto thee.

50 For now the most High seeth that thou art grieved unfeignedly, and sufferest from *thy* whole heart for her, so hath he shewed thee the brightness of her glory, and the comeliness of her beauty:
Precept: Feignedly/Feigned = *Ridiculously, Pretend: Jeremiah 3:10 | 1 Samuel 21:13 | 2 Samuel 14:2 | Psalm 17:1*

51 and therefore I bade thee remain in the field where no house was builded:

52 For I knew that the Highest would shew this unto thee.

53 Therefore I commanded thee to go into the field, where no foundation of *any* building was.

54 For in the place wherein the Highest beginneth to shew his city, there can no man's building be able to stand.

55 *And* therefore fear not, let not thine heart be affrighted, but go *thy way* in, and see the beauty and greatness of the building, as much as thine eyes be able to see:

56 and then shalt thou hear as much as thine ears may comprehend.
Precept: Comprehend = *Understand: Job 37:5 | Isaiah 44:18 | Sirach/Ecclesiasticus 32:8*

57 For thou art blessed above many *other,* and art called with the

Highest; and so *are but* few.

*Precept: **Blessed*** *= Knowledge of God, All things, Giving knowledge of, Works, The Heavenly Gift of Knowledge, give understanding and knowledge of Blessed = Hallowed, Joined to, Joined, Give, Joined together, Gave knowledge to, Commanded , Praised, Holy, Render, Named Bless = Worship, Give, will Give, Will give you, give us a, praise, Nehemiah 9:5 | Genesis 1:22 | Psalm 33:12 | 2 Esdras 13:24*

58 But to morrow at night thou shalt remain here;

59 and *so* shall the Highest shew thee visions of the high *things,* which the most High will do unto them that dwell upon the earth in the last days. So I slept that night and another, like as he commanded me.

2 ESDRAS CHAPTER 11

1 Then saw I a dream, and, behold, there came up from the sea an eagle, which had twelve feathered wings, and three heads.
Precept: Deuteronomy 28:49

2 And I saw, and, behold, she spread her wings over all the earth, and all the winds of the air blew on her, and were gathered together.

3 And I beheld, and out of her feathers there grew *other* contrary feathers; and they became little feathers and small.
Precept: Contrary = A fact, Opposite, being different or opposite extremes: Leviticus 26:28, 41 | Ezekiel 16:34 | 2 Esdras 11:3 | Wisdom 15:7 | Matthew 14:24

4 But her heads were at rest: the head in the midst was greater than the other, yet rested it with the residue.

5 Moreover I beheld, and, lo, the eagle flew with her feathers, and reigned upon earth, and over them that dwelt therein.

6 And I saw that all *things* under heaven were subject unto her, and no man spake against her, no, not one creature upon earth.
Precept: Heaven = Firmament Separated from he earth. The color blue of the sky was attributed to the chaotic waters that the firmament is separated: Genesis 1:7 | Deuteronomy 5:8 | Job 26:11 | 2 Samuel 22:8

7 And I beheld, and, lo, the eagle rose upon her talons, and spake to her feathers, saying,

8 Watch not all at once: sleep every one in his own place, and watch by course:

9 but let the heads be preserved for the last.

10 And I beheld, and, lo, the voice went not out of her heads, but from the midst of her body.

11 And I numbered her contrary feathers, and, behold, there were eight of them.

Precept: Contrary = *A fact, Opposite, being different or opposite extremes: Leviticus 26:28, 41 | Ezekiel 16:34 | 2 Esdras 11:3 | Wisdom 15:7 | Matthew 14:24*

12 And I looked, and, behold, on the right side there arose one feather, and reigned over all the earth;

13 and so it was, *that* when it reigned, the end of it came, and the place thereof appeared no more: so the *next* following stood up. and reigned, and had a great time;

14 And it happened, that when it reigned, the end of it came *also*, like as the first, so that it appeared no more.

15 Then came there a voice unto it, and said,

16 Hear thou that hast borne rule over the earth so long: this I say unto thee, before thou beginnest to appear no more,

17 There shall none after thee attain unto thy time, neither unto the half thereof.

18 Then arose the third, and reigned as the other before, and appeared no more also.

19 So went it with all the residue one after another, as that *every one* reigned, and then appeared no more.

20 Then I beheld, and, lo, in process of time the feathers that followed stood up upon the right side, that they might rule also; and *some* of them ruled, but within a while they appeared no more:

21 for some of them were set up, but ruled not.

22 After this I looked, and, behold, *the* twelve feathers appeared no more, nor the two little feathers:

23 and there was no more upon the eagle's body, but three heads that rested, and six little wings.

24 Then saw I also that two little feathers divided themselves from the six, and remained under the head that was upon the right side: for the four continued in their place.

25 And I beheld, and, lo, *the feathers that were* under the wing thought to set up themselves and to have the rule.

26 And I beheld, and, lo, there was one set up, but shortly it appeared no more.

27 And the second was sooner away than the first.

28 And I beheld, and, lo, the two that remained thought also in themselves to reign:

29 and when they so thought, behold, there awaked one of the heads that were at rest, *namely, it* that was in the midst; for that was greater than the two *other* heads.

30 And *then* I saw that the two *other* heads were joined with it.

31 And, behold, the head was turned with them that were with it, and did eat up the two *feathers* under the wing that would have reigned.

32 But this head put the whole earth in fear, and bare rule in it over *all* those that dwelt upon the earth with much oppression; and it had the governance of the world more than all the wings

that had been.

33 And after this I beheld, and, lo, the head *that was* in the midst suddenly appeared no more, like as the wings.

34 But there remained the two heads, which also in like sort ruled upon the earth, and over those that dwelt therein.

35 And I beheld, and, lo, the head upon the right side devoured it that *was* upon the left *side*.

36 Then I head a voice, which said unto me, Look before thee, and consider *the thing* that thou seest.

37 And I beheld, and lo, as it were a roaring lion chased out of the wood: and I saw that he sent out a man's voice unto the eagle, and said,

38 Hear thou, I will talk with thee, and the Highest shall say unto thee,

39 Art not thou *it* that remainest of the four beasts, whom I made to reign in my world, that the end of their times might come through them?
Precept: Daniel 7:3

40 And the fourth came, and overcame all the beasts that were past, and had power over the world with great fearfulness, and over the whole compass of the earth with much wicked oppression; and so long time dwelt he upon the earth with deceit.
Precept: Daniel 7:7, 19, 23; 2:40

41 For the earth hast thou not judged with truth.

42 For thou hast afflicted the meek, thou hast hurt the peaceable, thou hast loved liars, and destroyed the dwellings of them that

brought forth fruit, and hast cast down the walls of such as did thee no harm.

43 Therefore is thy wrongful dealing come up unto the Highest, and thy pride unto the Mighty.

44 The Highest also hath looked upon the proud times, and, behold, they are ended, and his abominations are fulfilled.

*Precept: **Abominations*** = *Repugnant, detestable act, person or thing. Corrupted, Polluted, Abhorrent, loathsome, unclean, and rejected; Most hated: Exodus 8:26 | Deuteronomy 7:25; 17:1; 18:12 | Proverbs 6:16; 20:23; 28:9 | Psalms 119:163 | Sirach/Ecclesiasticus 13:20; 20:8 | Amos 5:10; 6:8*

45 *And* therefore appear no more, thou eagle, nor thy horrible wings, nor thy wicked feathers nor thy malicious heads, nor thy hurtful claws, nor all thy vain body:

46 that all the earth may be refreshed, and may return, being delivered from thy violence, and *that* she may hope for the judgment and mercy of him that made her.

2 ESDRAS CHAPTER 12

1 And it came to pass, whiles the lion spake these words unto the eagle, I saw,

2 and, behold, the head that remained and the four wings appeared no more, and the two went unto it and set themselves up to reign, and their kingdom was small, and fill of uproar.

3 And I saw, and, behold, they appeared no more, and the whole body of the eagle was burnt so that the earth was in great fear: then awaked I out of the trouble and trance of *my* mind, and from great fear, and said unto my spirit,

4 Lo, this hast thou done unto me, in that thou searchest out the ways of the Highest.

5 Lo, yet am I weary in *my* mind, and very weak in my spirit; and little strength is there in me, for the great fear wherewith I was afflicted this night.

6 Therefore will I now beseech the Highest, that he will comfort me unto the end.

7 And I said, Lord that bearest rule, if I have found grace before thy sight, and if I am justified with thee before many *others*, and if my prayer indeed be come up before thy face;

8 comfort me *then*, and shew me thy servant the interpretation and plain difference of this fearful vision, that thou mayest perfectly comfort my soul.

Precept: Interpretation = *A clear explanation from the language from which it came: Genesis 40:5, 12, 18 | Judges 7:15 | Isaiah 36:11 | Daniel 2:1-11; 2:24-49 | Of Tongues: 1 Corinthians 14:26-28 |* **False Biblical** *Interpretations are done using* **Theology, Hermeneutics, Exegesis,** *and* **Inductive study methods:** *Ecclesiastes 12:12*

9 For thou hast judged me worthy to shew me the last times.

10 And he said unto me, This is the interpretation of the vision:
Precept: Interpretation = A clear explanation from the language from which it came using precepts of scripture: Genesis 40:5, 12, 18 | Judges 7:15 | Isaiah 36:11 | Daniel 2:1-11; 2:24-49 | Isaiah 28:10 | Psalm 199:4; 104 | Of Tongues: 1 Corinthians 14:26-28 | False Biblical Interpretations are done using Theology, Hermeneutics, Exegesis, and Inductive study methods: Ecclesiastes 12:12

11 The eagle, whom thou sawest come up from the sea, is the kingdom which was seen in the vision of thy brother Daniel.
Precept: Daniel 7:7

12 But it was not expounded unto him, therefore now I declare *it* unto thee.

13 Behold, the days will come, that there shall rise up a kingdom upon earth, and it shall be feared above all the kingdoms that were before it.

14 In the same shall twelve kings reign, one after another:

15 whereof the second shall begin to reign, and shall have more time than *any of* the twelve.

16 *And* this do the twelve wings signify, which thou sawest.

17 As for the voice which thou heardest speak, *and that thou sawest* not to go out from the heads but from the midst of the body thereof, this is the interpretation:
Precept: Interpretation = A clear explanation from the language from which it came using precepts of scripture: Genesis 40:5, 12, 18 | Judges 7:15 | Isaiah 36:11 | Daniel 2:1-11; 2:24-49 | Isaiah 28:10 | Psalm 199:4; 104 | Of Tongues: 1 Corinthians 14:26-28 | False Biblical Interpretations are done using Theology, Hermeneutics, Exegesis, and Inductive study methods: Ecclesiastes 12:12

18 That after the time of that kingdom there shall arise great strivings, and it shall stand in peril of failing: nevertheless it shall

not then fall, but shall be restored again to his beginning.

19 And whereas thou sawest the eight *small* under feathers sticking to her wings, this is the interpretation:

Precept: Interpretation = *A clear explanation from the language from which it came using precepts of scripture: Genesis 40:5, 12, 18 | Judges 7:15 | Isaiah 36:11 | Daniel 2:1-11; 2:24-49 | Isaiah 28:10 | Psalm 199:4; 104 | Of Tongues: 1 Corinthians 14:26-28 |* **False Biblical** *Interpretations are done using* **Theology**, **Hermeneutics**, **Exegesis**, *and* **Inductive study methods:** *Ecclesiastes 12:12*

20 *That* in him there shall arise eight kings, whose times shall be *but* small, and *their* years swift.

21 And two of them shall perish, the middle time approaching: four shall be kept until their end begin to approach: but two shall be kept unto the end.

22 And whereas thou sawest three heads resting, this is the interpretation:

Precept: Interpretation = *A clear explanation from the language from which it came using precepts of scripture: Genesis 40:5, 12, 18 | Judges 7:15 | Isaiah 36:11 | Daniel 2:1-11; 2:24-49 | Isaiah 28:10 | Psalm 199:4; 104 | Of Tongues: 1 Corinthians 14:26-28 |* **False Biblical** *Interpretations are done using* **Theology**, **Hermeneutics**, **Exegesis**, *and* **Inductive study methods:** *Ecclesiastes 12:12*

23 In his last *days* shall the most High raise up three kingdoms, and renew many *things* therein, and they shall have the dominion of the earth,

24 and *of those* that dwell therein, with much oppression, above all *those* that were before them: therefore are they called the heads of the eagle.

25 For these are they that shall accomplish his wickedness, and that shall finish his last *end.*

26 And whereas thou sawest that the great head appeared no more, it signifieth that one of them shall die upon his bed, and

yet with pain.

27 For the two that remain shall be slain with the sword.

28 For the sword of the one shall devour the other: but at the last shall he fall through the sword himself.

29 And whereas thou sawest two *feathers* under the wings passing over the head that is on the right side;

30 it signifieth that these are they, whom the Highest hath kept unto their end: this is the small kingdom and full of trouble, as thou sawest.

31 And the lion, whom thou sawest rising up out of the wood, and roaring, and speaking to the eagle, and rebuking her for her unrighteousness with all the words which thou hast heard;
*Precept: **Unrighteousness** = Sin, Wickedness, Injustice, violation of the divine law of God, Ungodly acts, Abomination(s), Fools building upon sand: Matthew 7:26 | Exodus 23:1 | Leviticus 19:15 | Deuteronomy 25:16 | Tobit 4:5; 12:8 | Wisdom 1:5 | Sirach/ Ecclesiasticus 7:3; 17:14*

32 this is the anointed, which the Highest hath kept *for* them and for their wickedness unto the end: he shall reprove them, and shall upbraid them with their cruelty.

33 For he shall set them *before him* alive in judgment, and shall rebuke them, and correct them.

34 For the rest of my people shall he deliver with mercy, *those* that have been pressed upon my borders, and he shall make them joyful until the coming of the day of judgment, whereof I have spoken unto thee from the beginning.

35 This *is* the dream that thou *sawest,* and these *are* the interpretations.
*Precept: **Interpretation** = A clear explanation from the language from which it came*

*using precepts of scripture: Genesis 40:5, 12, 18 | Judges 7:15 | Isaiah 36:11 | Daniel 2:1-11; 2:24-49 | Isaiah 28:10 | Psalm 199:4; 104 | Of Tongues: 1 Corinthians 14:26-28 | **False Biblical** Interpretations are done using **Theology**, **Hermeneutics**, **Exegesis**, and **Inductive study methods**: Ecclesiastes 12:12*

36 Thou only hast been meet to know this secret of the Highest.

37 Therefore write all these *things* that thou hast seen in a book, and hide them:
Precept: *Revelation 1:19*

38 and teach them to the wise of the people, whose hearts thou knowest may comprehend and keep these secrets.
Precept: Comprehend = *Understand: Job 37:5 | Isaiah 44:18 | Sirach/Ecclesiasticus 32:8*

39 But wait thou here thyself yet seven days more, that it may be shewed thee, whatsoever it pleaseth the Highest to declare unto thee. And *with that* he went his way.

40 And it came to pass, when all the people saw that the seven days were past, and I not come again into the city, they gathered them all together, from the least unto the greatest, and came unto me, and said,

41 What have we offended thee? and what evil have we done against thee, that thou forsakest us, and sittest *here* in this place?

42 For of all the prophets thou only art left us, as a cluster of the vintage, and as a candle in a dark place, and as a haven or ship preserved from the tempest.

43 Are not the evils which are come to us sufficient?

44 If thou shalt forsake us, how much better had it been for us, if we also had been burned in the midst of Sion?

45 For we are not better than they that died there. And they wept with a loud voice. Then answered I them, and said,

46 Be of good comfort, O Israel; and be not heavy, thou house of Jacob:

*Precept: Israel = IZ-ray-el; means: A prince of God | **Jacob** = JAY-kuhb; means: Supplants*

47 For the Highest hath you in remembrance, and the Mighty hath not forgotten you in temptation.

48 As for me, I have not forsaken you, neither am I departed from you: but am come into this place, to pray for the desolation of Sion, *and* that I might seek mercy for the low estate of your sanctuary.

*Precept: Desolation = DES-O-lation = Loneliness, Sadness, Devastation, Ruin. Also called **Desolate**: Genesis 47:19 | Leviticus 26:34-35 | Isaiah 13:9 | 1 Esdras 1:58; 2:23*

49 And now go *your way* home every man, and after these days will I come unto you.

50 So the people went their way into the city, like as I commanded them:

51 But I remained still in the field seven days, as *the angel* commanded me; and did eat only in those days of the flowers of the field, *and* had my meat of the herbs.

Precept: Angel = appear in a dream is a spirit angel. And angel appear in the flesh is an messenger of the flesh (A Nazarite, vowed to God, many times) of God: Matthew 2:13, 19 in a dream | Genesis 31:11

2 ESDRAS CHAPTER 13

1 And it came to pass after seven days, I dreamed a dream by night:

2 and, lo, there arose a wind from the sea, that it moved all the waves thereof.

3 And I beheld, and, lo, that man waxed strong with the thousands of heaven: and when he turned his countenance to look, all *the things* trembled that were seen under him.
Precept: Heaven = Firmament Separated from he earth. The color blue of the sky was attributed to the chaotic waters that the firmament is separated: Genesis 1:7 | Deuteronomy 5:8 | Job 26:11 | 2 Samuel 22:8

4 And whensoever the voice went out of his mouth, all they burned that heard his voice, like as the earth faileth when it feeleth the fire.

5 And after this I beheld, and, lo, there was gathered together a multitude of men, out of number, from the four winds of the heaven, to subdue the man that came out of the sea
Precept: Heaven = Firmament Separated from he earth. The color blue of the sky was attributed to the chaotic waters that the firmament is separated: Genesis 1:7 | Deuteronomy 5:8 | Job 26:11 | 2 Samuel 22:8

6 But I beheld, and, lo, he had graved himself a great mountain, and flew up upon it.

7 But I would have seen the region or place whereout the hill was graven, and I could not.

8 And after this I beheld, and, lo, all they which were gathered together to subdue him were sore afraid, *and* yet durst fight.

9 And, lo, as he saw the violence of the multitude that came, he neither lifted up his hand, nor held sword, nor any instrument of

war:

10 but only I saw that he sent out of his mouth as it had been a blast of fire, and out of his lips a flaming breath, and out of his tongue he cast out sparks and tempests.

11 And they were all mixed together; the blast of fire, the flaming breath, and the great tempest; and fell with violence upon the multitude which was prepared to fight, and burned them up every one, so that upon a sudden of an innumerable multitude nothing was to be perceived, but only dust and smell of smoke: when I saw *this* I was afraid.

12 Afterward saw I the same man come down from the mountain, and call unto him another peaceable Multitude.

13 And there came much people unto him, whereof some were glad, some were sorry, and some *of them* were bound, *and* other some brought of them that were offered: then was I sick through great fear, and I awaked, and said,

14 Thou hast shewed thy servant these wonders from the beginning, and hast counted me worthy that thou shouldest receive my prayer:

15 shew me now yet the interpretation of this dream.
Precept: Interpretation = *A clear explanation from the language from which it came using precepts of scripture: Genesis 40:5, 12, 18 | Judges 7:15 | Isaiah 36:11 | Daniel 2:1-11; 2:24-49 | Isaiah 28:10 | Psalm 199:4; 104 | Of Tongues: 1 Corinthians 14:26-28 |* **False Biblical** *Interpretations are done using* **Theology, Hermeneutics, Exegesis,** *and* **Inductive study methods:** *Ecclesiastes 12:12*

16 For as I conceive in mine understanding, woe *unto them* that shall be left in those days and much more woe *unto them* that are not left behind!

17 For *they* that were not left were in heaviness.

18 Now understand I *the things* that are laid up in the latter days, which shall happen unto them, and to those that are left behind.

19 Therefore are they come into great perils and many necessities, like as these dreams declare.
Precept: Perils = *Risk of being injured, Destroyed, or Lost, Risk: Lamentations 5:9 | Sirach/Ecclesiasticus 13:13 | 2 Maccabees 1:11 | Romans 8:35 | 2 Timothy 3:1*

20 Yet is it easier for him that is in danger to come into these *things*, than to pass away as a cloud out of the world, and not to see *the things* that happen in the last days. And he answered unto me, and said,

21 The interpretation of the vision shall I shew thee, and I will open unto thee *the thing* that thou hast required.
Precept: Interpretation = *A clear explanation from the language from which it came using precepts of scripture: Genesis 40:5, 12, 18 | Judges 7:15 | Isaiah 36:11 | Daniel 2:1-11; 2:24-49 | Isaiah 28:10 | Psalm 199:4; 104 | Of Tongues: 1 Corinthians 14:26-28 |* **False Biblical** *Interpretations are done using* **Theology, Hermeneutics, Exegesis,** *and* **Inductive study methods:** *Ecclesiastes 12:12*

22 Whereas thou hast spoken of them that are left behind, this is the interpretation:
Precept: Interpretation = *A clear explanation from the language from which it came using precepts of scripture: Genesis 40:5, 12, 18 | Judges 7:15 | Isaiah 36:11 | Daniel 2:1-11; 2:24-49 | Isaiah 28:10 | Psalm 199:4; 104 | Of Tongues: 1 Corinthians 14:26-28 |* **False Biblical** *Interpretations are done using* **Theology, Hermeneutics, Exegesis,** *and* **Inductive study methods:** *Ecclesiastes 12:12*

23 He that shall endure the peril in that time hath kept himself: they that be fallen into danger are such as have works, and faith toward the Almighty.
Precept: Faith = *The Spirit of Belief, or the spirit of the believer (Holy Spirit): Galatians 3:6, 24-25 | Jonah 3:5 | Judith 14:10 | John 6:29 | Romans 3:3, 22; 4:3 | James 2:23 | 1 Peter 1:21 |* **Peril** = *Risk of being injured, Destroyed, or Lost, Risk: Lamentations 5:9 | Sirach/Ecclesiasticus 13:13 | 2 Maccabees 1:11 | Romans 8:35 | 2 Timothy 3:1*

24 Know *this* therefore, that *they* which *be* left behind are more

blessed than they that be dead.

Precept: Blessed = *Knowledge of God, All things, Giving knowledge of, Works, The Heavenly Gift of Knowledge, give understanding and knowledge of Blessed = Hallowed, Joined to, Joined, Give, Joined together, Gave knowledge to, Commanded, Praised, Holy, Render, Named Bless = Worship, Give, will Give, Will give you, give us a, praise, Nehemiah 9:5 | Genesis 1:22 | Psalm 33:12 | 2 Esdras 13:24*

25 This *is* the meaning of the vision: Whereas thou sawest a man coming up from the midst of the sea:

26 the same is he whom *God* the Highest hath kept a great season, which by his own self shall deliver his creature: and he shall order *them* that are left behind.

27 And whereas thou sawest, that out of his mouth there came as a blast *of wind*, and fire, and storm;

28 and that he held neither sword, nor *any* instrument of war, but that the rushing in of him destroyed the *whole* multitude that came to subdue him; this is the interpretation:

Precept: Interpretation = *A clear explanation from the language from which it came using precepts of scripture: Genesis 40:5, 12, 18 | Judges 7:15 | Isaiah 36:11 | Daniel 2:1-11; 2:24-49 | Isaiah 28:10 | Psalm 199:4; 104 | Of Tongues: 1 Corinthians 14:26-28 | False Biblical Interpretations are done using Theology, Hermeneutics, Exegesis, and Inductive study methods: Ecclesiastes 12:12*

29 Behold, the days come, when the most High will begin to deliver them that are upon the earth.

30 And he shall come to the astonishment of them that dwell on the earth.

31 And one shall undertake to fight against another, one city against another, one place against another, one people against another, and one realm against another.

32 And *the time* shall be when these *things* shall come to pass, and the signs shall happen which I shewed thee before, and then

shall my Son be declared, whom thou sawest as a man ascending.
Precept: Declared = *Made known, Promised, Manifested: Daniel 4:18 | 2 Esdras 14:35 | 1 Corinthians 3:13 | Declared: Leviticus 23:44 | Deuteronomy 4:13 | Job 26:3 | 1 Esdras 2:24; 3:16 | 2 Esdras 4:4; 6:28 | Tobit 10:8; 13:4 | Judith 8:34; 10:13 |*

33 And when all the people hear his voice, every man shall in their own land leave the battle they have one against another.

34 And an innumerable multitude shall be gathered together, as *thou sawest them*, willing to come, and to overcome him by fighting.

35 But he shall stand upon the top of the mount Sion.

36 And Sion shall come, and shall be shewed to all *men*, being prepared and builded, like as thou sawest the hill graven without hands.

37 And this my Son shall rebuke the wicked inventions of those nations, which for their wicked life are fallen into the tempest;

38 *and shall lay before them* their evil thoughts, and the torments wherewith they shall begin to be tormented, which are like unto a flame: and he shall destroy them without labour by the law which is like unto fire.

39 And whereas thou sawest that he gathered another peaceable multitude unto him;

40 those are the ten tribes, which were carried *away* prisoners out of their own land in the time of Osea the king, whom Salmanasar the king of Assyria led away captive, and he carried them over the waters, and *so* came they into another land.
Precept: Assyria = *uh-SIHR-ih-uh. Ancient empire seen as the symbol of terror and tyranny. Assyria received its name from the tiny city-state Asshur, on the western bank of the Tigris River in the northern Mesopotamia (modern Iraq). The Hebrew name occurs frequently in the scriptures and translated Assyria you will see (Genesis 2;14),*

*Assur (Ezra 4:2 and Psalm 83:8) | **Osea** = oh-SEE-uh, is Greek. The Hebrew translation is Hoshea = how-SHEE-uh; means: Salvation: Numbers 13:8 | **Salamasar** = sal-ma-na-sar*

41 But they took this counsel among themselves, that they would leave the multitude of the heathen, and go forth into a further country, where never mankind dwelt,

42 that *they* might there keep their statutes, which they never kept in their own land.

43 And they entered into Euphrates by the narrow places of the river.
Precept: Euphrates *= yoo-FRAY-teez; means: The good and abounding river*

44 For the most High then shewed signs for them, and held still the flood, till they were passed over.

45 For through that country there was a great way to go, *namely*, of a year and a half: and the same region is called Arsareth.
Precept: Arsareth *= AHR-suh-reth*

46 Then dwelt they there until the latter time; and now when they shall begin to come,

47 the Highest shall stay the springs of the stream again, that they may go through: therefore sawest thou the multitude with peace.

48 But *those* that be left behind of thy people are they that are found within my borders.

49 Now when he destroyeth the multitude of the nations that are gathered together, he shall defend his people that remain.

50 And then shall he shew them great wonders.

51 Then said I, O Lord that bearest rule, shew me this: Wherefore have I seen the man coming up from the midst of the sea?

52 And he said unto me, Like as thou canst neither seek out nor know *the things* that are in the deep of the sea: *even* so can no man upon earth see my Son, or those that be with him, but in the day time.

53 This is the interpretation of the dream which thou sawest, and whereby thou only art here lightened.
Precept: Interpretation = *A clear explanation from the language from which it came using precepts of scripture: Genesis 40:5, 12, 18 | Judges 7:15 | Isaiah 36:11 | Daniel 2:1-11; 2:24-49 | Isaiah 28:10 | Psalm 199:4; 104 | Of Tongues: 1 Corinthians 14:26-28 | **False Biblical** Interpretations are done using **Theology**, **Hermeneutics**, **Exegesis**, and **Inductive study methods:** Ecclesiastes 12:12*

54 For thou hast forsaken thine own *way*, and applied thy diligence unto my law, and sought *it*.

55 Thy life hast thou ordered in wisdom, and hast called understanding thy mother.

56 And therefore have I shewed thee the treasures of the Highest: after other three days I will speak other *things* unto thee, and declare unto thee mighty and wondrous *things*.

57 Then went I forth into the field, giving praise and thanks greatly unto the most High because of *his* wonders which he did in time;

58 and because he governeth the same, and such *things* as fall in *their* seasons: and there I sat three days.

2 ESDRAS CHAPTER 14

1 And it came to pass upon the third day, I sat under an oak, and, behold, there came a voice out of a bush over against me, and said, Esdras, Esdras.

Precept: Esdras = *Ez-druhs, is Greek. The Hebrew translation is* **Ezra** = *Ez-ruh; means: Yahawah is my help*

2 And I said, Here *am* I, Lord And I stood up upon my feet.

3 Then said he unto me, In the bush I did manifestly reveal myself unto Moses, and talked with him, when my people served in Egypt:

4 and I sent him and led my people out of Egypt, and brought him up to the mount of where I held him by me a long season,

5 and told him many wondrous *things*, and shewed him the secrets of the times, and the end; and commanded him, saying,

6 These words shalt thou declare, and these shalt thou hide.

7 And now I say unto thee,

8 That thou lay up in thy heart the signs that I have shewed, and the dreams that thou hast seen, and the interpretations which thou hast heard:

Precept: Interpretation = *A clear explanation from the language from which it came using precepts of scripture: Genesis 40:5, 12, 18 | Judges 7:15 | Isaiah 36:11 | Daniel 2:1-11; 2:24-49 | Isaiah 28:10 | Psalm 199:4; 104 | Of Tongues: 1 Corinthians 14:26-28 |* **False Biblical** *Interpretations are done using* **Theology, Hermeneutics, Exegesis,** *and* **Inductive study methods:** *Ecclesiastes 12:12*

9 for thou shalt be taken away from all, *and* from henceforth thou shalt remain with my Son, and with such as be like thee, until the times be ended.

10 For the world hath lost his youth, and the times begin to wax old.

11 For the world is divided into twelve parts, and the ten *parts* of it are gone *already*, and half of a tenth part:
Precept: *1 Kings 11:31-32 | Genesis 49:28 | Ezekiel 47:13 | Sirach/Ecclesiasticus 44:23 | Matthew 19:28 | Luke 22:30 | Acts 26:7 | James 1:1 | 2 Esdras 5:23-28*

12 and there remaineth *that which is* after the half of the tenth part.

13 Now therefore set thine house in order, and reprove thy people, comfort such of them as be in trouble, and now renounce corruption,
Precept: **Corruption** = *Decay, Decomposition, Sinfulness, Decay life: Isaiah 1:4 | Leviticus 22:24-25 | Psalm 14:1 | Jeremiah 6:28 | Wisdom 14:12, 25 | Sirach/ Ecclesiasticus 28:6; 31:5*

14 let go from thee mortal thoughts, cast away the burdens of man, put off now the weak nature,

15 And set aside the thoughts *that are* most heavy unto thee, and haste thee to flee from these times.

16 For yet greater evils than those which thou hast seen happen shall be done *hereafter*.

17 For *look* how much the world shall be weaker through age, so much *the more* shall evils increase upon them that dwell therein.

18 For the time is fled far away, and leasing is hard at hand: for now hasteth the vision to come, which thou hast seen.

19 Then answered I before thee, and said,

20 Behold, Lord, I will go, as thou hast commanded me, and reprove the people which are present: but *they* that shall be born

afterward, who shall admonish *them?* thus the world is set in darkness, and *they* that dwell therein *are* without light.

21 For thy law is burnt, therefore no man knoweth *the things* that are done of thee, or the work that shall begin.

22 But if I have found grace before thee, send the Holy Ghost into me, and I shall write all that hath been done in the world since the beginning, which were written in thy law, that men may find *thy* path, and *that they* which will live in the latter *days* may live.

23 And he answered me, saying, Go *thy way*, gather the people together, and say unto them, that they seek thee not for forty days.

24 But look thou prepare thee many box trees, and take with thee Sarea, Dabria, Selemia, Ecanus, and Asiel, these five which are ready to write swiftly;
Precept: Sarea = SEHR-eee-uh | *Dabria* = DAB-rih-uh | *Selemia* = sel-uh-MIGH-uh | *Ecanus* = ih-KAY-nuhs | *Asiel* = ASS-ih-uhl

25 and come hither, and I shall light a candle of understanding in thine heart, which shall not be put out, till *the things* be performed which thou shalt begin to write.

26 And when thou hast done, some things shalt thou publish, *and* some *things* shalt thou shew secretly to the wise: to morrow this hour shalt thou begin to write.

27 Then went I forth, as he commanded, and gathered all the people together, and said,

28 Hear these words, O Israel.
Precept: Israel = IZ-ray-el; means: A prince of God: Deuteronomy 5:1

29 Our fathers at the beginning were strangers in Egypt, from whence they were delivered:

30 and received the law of life, which they kept not, which ye also have transgressed after them.

31 Then was the land, even the land of Sion, parted among you by lot: but your fathers, and ye *yourselves,* have done unrighteousness, and have not kept the ways which the Highest commanded you.
Precept: Unrighteousness = Sin, Wickedness, Injustice, violation of the divine law of God, Ungodly acts, Abomination(s), Fools building upon sand: Matthew 7:26 | Exodus 23:1 | Leviticus 19:15 | Deuteronomy 25:16 | Tobit 4:5; 12:8 | Wisdom 1:5 | Sirach/ Ecclesiasticus 7:3; 17:14

32 And forasmuch as he is a righteous judge, he took from you in time *the thing* that he had given *you.*

33 And now are ye here, and your brethren among you.
Precept: Brethren = breth-ran: means: Referring to the members of a Sect, society, or of Profession. Many times used as Brother: Genesis 9:22, 25; 19:7 | Deuteronomy 3:20; 10:9 | 1 Esdras 8:47 | Tobit 1:3

34 Therefore if so be that ye will subdue your own understanding, and reform your hearts, ye shall be kept alive and after death ye shall obtain mercy.

35 For after death shall the judgment come, when we shall live again: and then shall the names of the righteous be manifest, and the works of the ungodly shall be declared.
Precept: Declared = Made known, Promised, Manifested: Daniel 4:18 | 2 Esdras 14:35 | 1 Corinthians 3:13 | Declared: Leviticus 23:44 | Deuteronomy 4:13 | Job 26:3 | 1 Esdras 2:24; 3:16 | 2 Esdras 4:4; 6:28 | Tobit 10:8; 13:4 | Judith 8:34; 10:13 |

36 Let no man therefore come unto me now, nor seek after me these forty days.

37 So I took the five men, as he commanded me, and we went

into the field, and remained there.

38 And the next day, behold, a voice called me, saying, Esdras, open thy mouth, and drink that I give thee to drink.
Precept: Esdras = *Ez-druhs, is Greek. The Hebrew translation is* **Ezra** = *Ez-ruh; means: Yahawah is my help*

39 Then opened I my mouth, and, behold, *he* reached me a full cup, which was full as it were with water, but the colour of it *was* like fire.

40 And I took *it*, and drank: and when I had drunk *of it*, my heart uttered understanding, and wisdom grew in my breast, for my spirit strengthened *my* memory:

41 and my mouth was opened, and shut no more.

42 The Highest gave understanding unto the five men, and they wrote the wonderful visions of the night that were told, which they knew not: *and they sat forty days, and they wrote in the day,* and at night they ate bread.

43 As for me. I spake in the day, and I held not my tongue by night.

44 In forty days *they* wrote two hundred and four books.

45 And it came to pass, when the forty days were filled, *that* the Highest spake, saying, The first that thou hast written publish openly, that the worthy and unworthy may read *it*:

46 but keep the seventy last, that thou mayest deliver them *only* to such as be wise among the people:

47 for in them is the spring of understanding, the fountain of wisdom, and the stream of knowledge.

48 And I did so.

2 ESDRAS CHAPTER 15

1 Behold, speak thou in the ears of my people the words of prophecy, which I will put in thy mouth, saith the Lord:
Precept: Deuteronomy 18:18

2 and cause them to be written in paper: for they are faithful and true.
Precept: Faith = *The Spirit of Belief, or the spirit of the believer (Holy Spirit): Galatians 3:6, 24-25 | Jonah 3:5 | Judith 14:10 | John 6:29 | Romans 3:3, 22; 4:3 | James 2:23 | 1 Peter 1:21*

3 Fear not the imaginations against thee, let not the incredulity of them trouble thee, that speak *against thee*.

4 For all the unfaithful shall die in their unfaithfulness.

5 Behold, saith the Lord, I will bring plagues upon the world; the sword, famine, death, and destruction.

6 For wickedness hath exceedingly polluted the whole earth, and their hurtful works are fulfilled.

7 Therefore saith the Lord,

8 I will hold my tongue no more as touching their wickedness, which they profanely commit, neither will I suffer *them* in those *things*, in which they wickedly exercise themselves: behold, the innocent and righteous blood crieth unto me, and the souls of the just complain continually.

9 *And therefore*, saith the Lord, I will surely avenge them, and receive unto me all the innocent blood from among them.

10 Behold, my people is led as a flock to the slaughter: I will not suffer them now to dwell in the land of Egypt:

11 But I will bring them with a mighty hand and a stretched out arm, and smite *Egypt* with plagues, as before, and will destroy all the land thereof.

12 Egypt shall mourn, and the foundation of it *shall be* smitten with the plague and punishment that God shall bring upon it.

13 They that till the ground shall mourn: for their seeds shall fail through the blasting and hail, and with a fearful constellation.

14 Woe to the world and *them* that dwell therein!

15 For the sword and their destruction draweth nigh, and one people shall stand up and fight against another, and swords in their hands.

16 For there shall be sedition among men, and invading one another; they shall not regard their kings nor princes, *and* the course of their actions *shall stand* in their power.

17 A man shall desire to go into a city, and shall not be able.

18 For because of their pride the cities shall be troubled, the houses shall be destroyed, and men shall be afraid.

19 A man shall have no pity upon his neighbour, but shall destroy their houses with the sword, and spoil their goods, because of the lack of bread, and *for* great tribulation.
Precept: Neighbour(s) = *One who is a fellow Israelite, Members of a community united by divine covenant, law, and teachings, the Israelites' obligations to Yahawah (God): Exodus 2:13; 19:6; 22:25-26 | Leviticus 19:13, 15-17 | Deuteronomy 15:7-11 | 1 Samuel 28:17*

20 Behold, saith God, I will call together all the kings of the earth to reverence me, which are from the rising *of the sun*, from

the south, from the east, and Libanus; to turn themselves one against another, and repay *the things* that they have done to them.
*Precept: Libanus is another form of saying **Lebanon**; means: To be white, or The white mountain of Syria (White meaning snow): Jeremiah 18:14*

21 Like as they do yet this day unto my chosen, so will I do *also*, and recompense in their bosom. Thus saith the Lord God;

22 My right hand shall not spare the sinners, and *my* sword shall not cease over them that shed innocent blood upon the earth.

23 The fire is gone forth from his wrath, and hath consumed the foundations of the earth, and the sinners, like the straw that is kindled.

24 Woe to them that sin, and keep not my commandments! saith the Lord.

25 I will not spare them: go your way, *ye* children, from the power, defile not my sanctuary.

26 For the Lord knoweth all them that sin against him, *and* therefore delivereth he them unto death and destruction.

27 For now are the plagues come upon the whole earth and ye shall remain in them: for God shall not deliver you, because ye have sinned against him.

28 Behold an horrible vision, and the appearance thereof from the east:

29 Where the nations of the dragons of Arabia shall come out with many chariots, and the multitude of them shall be carried as the wind upon earth, that all *they* which hear them may fear and tremble.
Precept: Arabia = uh-RAY-bih-uh

30 Also the Carmanians raging in wrath shall go forth as the wild boars of the wood, and with great power shall they come, and join battle with them, and shall waste a portion of the land of the Assyrians.

Precept: Carmanians = *kar-mo-ni-anz: The residents of Carmania*

31 And then shall the dragons have the upper hand, remembering their nature; and *if* they shall turn themselves, conspiring together in great power to persecute them,

32 *then* these shall be troubled bled, and keep silence through their power, and shall flee.

33 And from the land of the Assyrians shall the enemy besiege them, and consume some of them, and in their host shall be fear and dread, and strife among their kings.

34 Behold clouds from the east and *from* the north unto the south, and they are very horrible to look upon, full of wrath and storm.

35 They shall smite one upon another, and they shall smite down a great multitude of stars upon the earth, even their own star; and blood shall be from the sword unto the belly,

36 and dung of men unto the camel's hough.

37 And there shall be great fearfulness and trembling upon earth: and *they* that see the wrath shall be afraid, and trembling shall come upon them.

38 And then shall there come great storms *from* the south, and from the north, and another part from the west.

39 And strong winds shall arise from the east, and shall open it; and the cloud which he raised up in wrath, and the star stirred to cause fear toward the east and west wind, shall be destroyed.

40 The great and mighty clouds shall be puffed up full of wrath, and the star, that they may make all the earth afraid, and them that dwell therein; and they shall pour out over every high and eminent place an horrible star,

41 fire, and hail, and flying swords, and many waters, that all fields may be full, and all rivers, with the abundance of great waters.

42 And they shall break down the cities and walls, mountains and hills, trees of the wood, and grass of the meadows, and their corn.

43 And they shall go stedfastly unto Babylon, and make her afraid.
Precept: Babylon = *Confuse, Confound; An enormously important city in antiquity ("gate of the god")*

44 They shall come to her, and besiege her, the star and all wrath shall they pour out upon her: then shall the dust and smoke go up unto the heaven, and all *they that be* about her shall bewail her.
Precept: Heaven = *Firmament Separated from he earth. The color blue of the sky was attributed to the chaotic waters that the firmament is separated: Genesis 1:7 | Deuteronomy 5:8 | Job 26:11 | 2 Samuel 22:8*

45 And *they* that remain under her shall do service unto them that have put *her* in fear.

46 And thou, Asia, *that art* partaker of the hope of Babylon, and *art* the glory of her person:
Precept: Babylon = *Confuse, Confound; An enormously important city in antiquity ("gate of the god")*

47 woe be unto thee, *thou* wretch, because thou hast made *thyself* like unto her; and hast decked thy daughters in whoredom, that *they* might please and glory in thy lovers, which have always desired to commit whoredom with thee.

48 Thou hast followed *her that is* hated in all her works and inventions: therefore saith God,

49 I will send plagues upon thee; widowhood, poverty, famine, sword, and pestilence, to waste thy houses with destruction and death.

50 And the glory of thy Power shall be dried up as a flower, the heat shall arise that is sent over thee.

51 Thou shalt be weakened as a poor woman with stripes, and *as one* chastised with wounds, so that the mighty and lovers shall not be able to receive thee.

52 Would I with jealousy have so proceeded against thee, saith the Lord,

53 if thou hadst not always slain my chosen, exalting the stroke of *thine* hands, and saying over their dead, when thou wast drunken,

54 Set forth the beauty of thy countenance?

55 The reward of thy whoredom *shall be* in thy bosom, therefore shalt thou receive recompence.

56 Like as thou hast done unto my chosen, saith the Lord, *even* so shall God do unto thee, and shall deliver thee into mischief

57 Thy children shall die of hunger, and thou shalt fall through

the sword: thy cities shall be broken down, and all thine shall perish with the sword in the field.

58 *They* that be in the mountains shall die of hunger, and eat their own flesh, and drink *their own* blood, for *very* hunger of bread, and thirst of water.

59 Thou *as* unhappy shalt come through the sea, and receive plagues again.

60 And in the passage they shall rush on the idle city, and shall destroy some portion of thy land, and consume part of thy glory, and shall return to Babylon that was destroyed.
Precept: Babylon = *Confuse, Confound; An enormously important city in antiquity ("gate of the god")*

61 And thou shalt be cast down by them as stubble, and they shall be unto thee *as* fire;

62 And shall consume thee, and thy cities, thy land, and thy mountains; all thy woods and *thy* fruitful trees shall they burn up with fire.

63 Thy children shall they carry *away* captive, and, *look*, what thou hast, they shall spoil it, and mar the beauty of thy face.

2 ESDRAS CHAPTER 16

1 Woe be unto thee, Babylon, and Asia! woe be unto thee, Egypt and Syria!

Precept: Babylon = Confuse, Confound; An enormously important city in antiquity ("gate of the god")

2 Gird up yourselves with cloths of sack and hair, bewail your children, and be sorry; for your destruction is at hand.

3 A sword is sent upon you, and who may turn it back?

4 a fire is sent among you, and who may quench it?

5 plagues are sent unto you, and what is he that may drive them away?

6 May any *s* drive away an hungry lion in the wood? or may *any one* quench the fire in stubble, when it hath begun to burn?

7 May one turn again the arrow that is shot of a strong archer?

8 The mighty Lord sendeth the plagues and who is he that can drive them away?

9 A fire shall go forth from his wrath, and who is he that may quench it?

10 He shall cast lightnings, and who shall not fear? he shall thunder, and who shall not be afraid?

11 The Lord shall threaten, and who shall not be utterly beaten to powder at his presence?

12 The earth quaketh, and the foundations thereof; the sea ariseth

up with waves from the deep, and the waves of it are troubled, and the fishes thereof *also*, before the Lord, and before the glory of his power:

13 for strong *is* his right hand that bendeth the bow, his arrows that he shooteth *are* sharp, *and* shall not miss, when they begin to be shot into the ends of the world.

14 Behold, the plagues are sent, and shall not return again, until they come upon the earth.

15 The fire is kindled, and shall not be put out, till it consume the foundation of the earth.

16 Like as an arrow which is shot of a mighty archer returneth not *backward: even* so the plagues that shall be sent upon earth shall not return *again*.

17 Woe is me! woe is me! who will deliver me in those days?

18 The beginning of sorrows and great mournings; the beginning of famine and great death; the beginning of wars, and the powers shall stand in fear; the beginning of evils! what shall I do when these evils shall come?

19 Behold, famine and plague, tribulation and anguish, are sent *as* scourges for amendment.

20 But for all these *things* they shall not turn from their wickedness, nor be always mindful of the scourges.

21 Behold, victuals shall be so good cheap upon earth, that they shall think themselves to be in good case, and *even* then shall evils grow upon earth, sword, famine, and great confusion.

22 For many *of them* that dwell upon earth shall perish of famine; and the other, that escape the hunger, shall the sword destroy.

23 And the dead shall be cast out as dung, and there shall be no man to comfort them: for the earth shall be wasted, and the cities shall be cast down.

24 There shall be no man left to till the earth, and to sow it

25 The trees shall give fruit, and who shall gather them?

26 The grapes shall ripen, and who shall tread them? for *all* places shall be desolate *of men*:

27 so that one man shall desire to see another, and to hear his voice.

28 For of a city there shall be ten left, and two of the field, which shall hide themselves in the thick groves, and in the clefts of the rocks.

29 As in an orchard of Olives upon every tree there are left three or four olives;

30 or as when a vineyard is gathered, there are left *some* clusters of them that diligently seek through the vineyard:

31 *even* so in those days there shall be three or four left by them that search their houses with the sword.

32 And the earth shall be laid waste, and the fields thereof shall wax old, and her ways and all her paths shall grow full of thorns, because no man shall travel therethrough.

33 The virgins shall mourn, having no bridegrooms; the women shall mourn, having no husbands; their daughters shall mourn, having no helpers.

34 In the wars shall their bridegrooms be destroyed, and their husbands shall perish of famine.

35 Hear now these *things* and understand them, *ye* servants of the Lord.

36 Behold, the word of the Lord, receive it: believe not the gods of whom the Lord spake.

37 Behold, the plagues draw nigh, and are not slack.

38 As when a woman with child in the ninth month bringeth forth her son, with two or three hours of her birth *great* pains compass her womb, which *pains*, when the child cometh forth, they slack not a moment:

39 *even* so shall not the plagues be slack to come upon the earth, and the world shall mourn, and sorrows shall come upon it on every side.

40 O my people, hear *my* word: make you ready to thy battle, and in *those* evils be even as pilgrims upon the earth.

41 He that selleth, *let him be* as he that fleeth *away*: and he that buyeth, as one that will lose:

42 he that occupieth merchandise, as he that hath no profit by *it*: and he that buildeth, as he that shall not dwell *therein*:

43 he that soweth, as if he should not reap: so also he that planteth the vineyard, as he that shall not gather the grapes:

44 they that marry, as they that shall get no children; and they that marry not, as the widowers.

45 *And* therefore they that labour labour in vain:

46 for strangers shall reap their fruits, and spoil their goods, overthrow *their* houses, and take their children captives, for in captivity and famine shall they get children.

47 And they that occupy their merchandise with robbery, the more they deck *their* cities, their houses, *their* possessions, and their own persons:

48 the more will I be angry with them for their sin, saith the Lord.

49 Like as a whore envieth a right honest and virtuous woman:

50 So shall righteousness hate iniquity, when she decketh herself, and shall accuse her to her face, when he cometh that shall defend him that *diligently* searcheth out every sin upon earth.

51 *And* therefore be ye not like thereunto, nor to the works thereof.

52 For yet a little, and iniquity shall be taken away out of the earth, and righteousness shall reign among you.

53 Let not the sinner say that he hath not sinned: for *God* shall burn coals of fire upon his head, which saith before the Lord God and his glory, I have not sinned.

54 Behold, the Lord knoweth all the works of men, their imaginations, their thoughts, and their hearts:

55 which spake *but* the word, Let the earth be made; and it was made: Let the heaven be made; and it was created.
Precept: Heaven = Firmament Separated from he earth. The color blue of the sky was attributed to the chaotic waters that the firmament is separated: Genesis 1:7 | Deuteronomy 5:8 | Job 26:11 | 2 Samuel 22:8 | Genesis 1:1 | Psalm 148:5

56 In his word were the stars made, and he knoweth the number of them.

57 He searcheth the deep, and the treasures thereof; he hath measured the sea, and what it containeth.

58 He hath shut the sea in the midst of the waters, and with his word hath he hanged the earth upon the waters.

59 He spreadeth out the heavens like a vault; upon the waters hath he founded it.
Precept: Heaven = Firmament Separated from he earth. The color blue of the sky was attributed to the chaotic waters that the firmament is separated: Genesis 1:7 | Deuteronomy 5:8 | Job 26:11 | 2 Samuel 22:8

60 In the desert hath he made springs of water, and pools upon the tops of the mountains, that the floods might pour down from the high rocks to water the earth.
Precept: Genesis 2:7

61 He made man, and put his heart in the midst of the body, and gave him breath, life, and understanding.

62 Yea and the Spirit of Almighty God, which made all *things*, and searcheth out all hidden *things* in the secrets of the earth,

63 *surely* he knoweth your inventions, and what ye think in your hearts, *even* them that sin, and would hide their sin.

64 Therefore hath the Lord exactly searched out all your works,

and he will put you all to shame.

65 And when your sins are brought forth, ye shall be ashamed before men, and *your own* sins shall be *your* accusers in that day.

66 What will ye do? or how will ye hide your sins before God and his angels?
Precept: Angel = appear in a dream is a spirit angel. And angel appear in the flesh is an messenger of the flesh (A Nazarite, vowed to God, many times) of God: Matthew 2:13, 19 in a dream | Genesis 31:11

67 Behold, God *himself* is the judge, fear him: leave off from your sins, and forget your iniquities, to meddle *no more* with them for ever: so shall God lead you forth, and deliver *you* from all trouble.

68 For, behold, the burning wrath of a great multitude is kindled over you, and they shall take *away* certain of you, and feed *you*, being idle, with things offered unto idols.

69 And *they* that consent unto them shall be had in derision and in reproach, and trodden under foot.
Precept: Derision = Mock, Scorn, laugh at, and Ridicule: Psalm 44:13; 79:4 | Ezekiel 23:32 | Hosea 7:16 | Job 30:1 | Wisdom 5:3

70 For there shall be in every place, and in the next cities, a great insurrection upon those that fear the Lord.

71 They shall be like mad *men*, sparing none, but still spoiling and destroying those that fear the Lord.

72 For they shall waste and take away *their* goods, and cast them out of their *houses.*

73 Then shall they be known, who are my chosen; and they shall be tried as the gold in the fire.

74 Hear, O *ye* my beloved, saith the Lord: behold, the days of trouble are at hand, but I will deliver you from the same.

75 Be ye not afraid neither doubt; for God is your guide,

76 and *the guide of them* who keep my commandments and precepts, saith the Lord God: let not your sins weigh you down, *and* let not your iniquities lift up themselves.

77 Woe *be unto them* that are bound with their sins, and covered with their iniquities like as a field is covered over with bushes, and the path thereof covered with thorns, that no man may travel through!

78 It is left undressed, and is cast into the fire to be consumed therewith.